FROM HAMBLEDON TO LORDS

Figure 1. Admission ticket signed by M. Lambert. The engraving is late eighteenth century.

FROM HAMBLEDON TO LORD'S

The Classics of Cricket

Edited by
John Arlott

Barry Shurlock

BARRY SHURLOCK & CO. (Publishers) Ltd
174 Stockbridge Road
WINCHESTER
Hants, SO22 6RW

© John Arlott, 1948 & 1975

First published, 1948
New edition, 1975

ISBN 0 903330 20 2

To
My Son, Jimmy
(1944–65)

Printed and bound in Great Britain by
REDWOOD BURN LIMITED
Trowbridge & Esher

Contents

List of Illustrations

Preface

THE PURPOSE OF THIS COLLECTION IS TO EVOKE, ILLUSTRATE AND AT least partly explain, a century of early cricket. The cricket of Hambledon is the starting point of this book. There was cricket before that, but it is ill documented. Haygarth's—unjustly called Lillywhite's—*Scores and Biographies* gives the scores of many earlier matches, codes of laws and random facts. Scores, though, while they may convey a picture of known players, cannot evoke an unknown scene. Much cricket writing is statistical or historical, relating facts in a way which does not create a picture or establish a perspective.

The period of the Hambledon Club, beginning about the middle of the eighteenth century, is the first phase of cricket of which any valid contemporary view exists. For this reason Hambledon has often carelessly and wrongly been called 'the cradle of cricket' when, in fact, the game had existed far earlier at important club level in Kent, Sussex and London. The picture is only dim for the next hundred years until the establishment of William Clarke's All England XI which has been argued as the beginning of modern cricket: in a strong link, W. G. Grace played against that team. In fact, the view consists almost entirely of that created by the three classical pieces of writing reproduced here. Between them John Nyren (with Charles Cowden Clarke as his amanuensis), the Rev. James Pycroft and the Rev. John Mitford provide an informed and often evocative, if sometimes thin, view of English cricket from the middle of the eighteenth century to the middle of the nineteenth.

William Denison in his *Sketches of the Players* affords the only other clear view of the period, but he is so specifically concerned with the round-arm bowling of Lillywhite and Broadbridge as to obscure perspective in detail and argument about the 'new throwing' bowling.

Nyren has been much reprinted and extracts especially from his 'Cricketers of My Time' (which is the section of his *The Young Cricketer's Tutor* reproduced here) have frequently been anthologised. The three have not, though, been collected in a single volume, except by E. V. Lucas in *The Hambledon Men* (Henry Frowde, 1907) which remains an outstanding work on early cricket. Carried out with Lucas's discerning taste and sympathetic editing, it is a complete and harmonious unity. The aim of *The Hambledon Men* was to illuminate the essentially eighteenth century story of the Hambledon Club. In this case it is to tell the story from that, the first remotely well documented period of cricket, to the All England XI.

Thus there is more here of Pycroft and Mitford on the later years than was necessary for E. V. Lucas's purpose. All three, in their different ways, are period characters, though Nyren has a greater literary stature—which may well be attributed to the hand of Clarke—than the other two. Nevertheless they form an effective unity in presenting the picture, not available anywhere else, of an age in a game then taking shape.

When this book was first published, in 1948, continuing wartime economies imposed low standards of paper and reproduction which this edition allows to be made good. Since then, too, there have been two further re-issues of Nyren's book. Each section has a separate introduction indicating the extent of editorial excision.

*Alresford,*1975   JOHN ARLOTT

ON JOHN NYREN'S

The Cricketers of my Time

∽✠∾

NO WORK ON CRICKET HAS BEEN MORE QUOTED THAN JOHN NYREN'S *The Cricketers of my Time* which was originally printed as "added to" his *The Young Cricketer's Tutor*, published by Effingham Wilson in 1833.

Eleven editions of the original book were issued and it has since been reprinted by Whibley, Sonnenschein, and E. V. Lucas.

Hambledon cricket club and its great players are seen at a range of forty years and through the rosy glass of nostalgia by an old man who had shared in their greatness. The title-page indicates that the matter was "collected and edited" by Charles Cowden Clarke. Clarke was an associate of Lamb which may well argue a true literary sensibility. Yet, in face of the evidence of his other writings it is difficult to believe that the high quality of the writing on Hambledon is to be attributed entirely to Clarke. Neither, on the available evidence, can any specific skill in writing be credited to Nyren. (As a result of his book he was invited to write an account of a cricket match which is disappointing in the extreme by any standard.) The most acceptable solution to the query posed by the production, by two extremely pedestrian writers, of a book which may be justifiably described as "inspired," seems to be that Nyren, in relating his experiences to Clarke, so communicated his own romantic enthusiasm that the writer retained it—in many of the original phrases. This self-contained section of the book is extremely short—it is, in fact, difficult to conceive of the intensity being maintained successfully over any substantially greater length. The first part of the volume, *The Young Cricketer's Tutor*, is deliberately excluded from this reprint not only because its aim (which is purely instructional) falls outside my scope, but because in style it cannot compare with the second section. The Dedication and Introduction, however, call for inclusion both because of their "period" quality and their sympathy with the text which follows. The introduction, signed C. C. C., is presumably Clarke's work—and in marked contrast to the remainder of the book.

Little can be said to extol this book which has not been said before, unless it be to indicate a setting which is too often and rather amazingly neglected. Nyren's cricketers have much in common with the people of Hardy's novels. Their country was the same, their origins the same and, because each of the writers himself belonged to the people of whom he wrote, these studies are among the few authentic peasant portraits in the language. It is arguable that this peasant strain is stronger than that of cricket in Nyren's cricketers : certainly it has an equal demand upon the sympathies of its editors. One modern editor, noting that Old John Small, recorded as a locally renowned violinist, was a member of the choir of Petersfield church (Haygarth, *Cricket Scores and Biographies*), assumes that he *sang* there. Had he known of that other musician, Old William Dewy, in Hardy's *Under the Greenwood Tree*, for so many years the bass-viol player in the Mellstock Church choir, he might have drawn a less hasty and sounder conclusion. The descendants of both Nyren's and Hardy's Wessex men, little changed from their fathers, still people Wessex : the old names still persist. Many of their characteristics are common to peasants anywhere in the world, others, however, are peculiarly those of the people that the first King of England ruled from Winchester. Nyren's is one of the very few books ever written on any game which can stand squarely upon its merits outside the literature of sport. *The Cricketers of my Time* is such a book because it comes out of a deep enthusiasm which had become a faith, a nostalgia which was as searching as intense, and a certainty which comes of knowing a game as a craft and one's fellow-practitioners as human beings. Few games-players, few men, combine these gifts. When we find the joint product of these qualities in print, it behoves us to recognise it with gratitude, and read it with sympathy that our delight may be savoured in recurring memories of a little empire of enthusiastic masters of a rare craft.

JOHN ARLOTT.

DEDICATION AND INTRODUCTION TO

THE YOUNG CRICKETER'S TUTOR

AND

THE CRICKETERS OF MY TIME

OR

RECOLLECTIONS OF THE MOST FAMOUS OLD PLAYERS

BY

JOHN NYREN

THE WHOLE COLLECTED AND EDITED

BY

CHARLES COWDEN CLARKE

Dedication

To WILLIAM WARD, Esq.

DEAR SIR,

You have kindly consented to my wish of dedicating my little book to you, and I am much pleased that you have done so : first, because you are a countryman of my own—having lived in Hampshire ; and secondly, and chiefly, because, as a CRICKETER, I consider you the most worthy man of the present day to reflect credit upon my choice as a patron.

It would ill become me, Sir, in this place to allude to other weighty reasons for congratulating myself upon this point—an insignificant book of instruction—as to the best mode of excelling in an elegant relaxation, not being the most fitting medium for digressing upon unquestionedly high public worth and integrity, or private condescension and amenity : at the same time, I cannot but feel how happily such a combination of qualities in a patron must redound to my own advantage.

I have not seen much of your playing—certainly not so much as I could have wished ; but so far as my observation and judgment extend, I may confidently pronounce you to be one of the safest players I remember to have seen. The circumstance of your rising so much above the ordinary standard in stature (your height, if I recollect, being six feet one inch), your extraordinary length of limb, your power and activity ; to all which, I may add, your perfect judgment of all points in the game ; have given you the superior advantages in play, and entitle you to the character I have given. As a proof of its correctness, the simple fact will suffice of your having gained the " longest hands " of any player upon record. This circumstance occurred upon the 24th and 25th July, 1820, at Mary-le-bone, when the great number of 278 runs appeared against your name, 108 more than any player ever gained ; and this, be it remembered, happened after the increase of the stumps in 1817.

May you long live, Sir, to foster and take your part in our favourite amusement ; and may you never relax your endeavours to restore the game to the good old principles from which, I regret to say, it has in some instances departed since the time I used to be an active member of the fraternity. You are aware that I principally allude to the practice that the modern bowlers have introduced of throwing the ball, although in direct infringement of a law prohibiting that action.

I beg to subscribe myself,

Dear Sir,

Your faithful Countryman,

And obedient humble Servant,

JOHN NYREN.

BROMLEY, MIDDLESEX.

March, 1833.

Introduction

꘏

O F ALL THE ENGLISH ATHLETIC GAMES, NONE, PERHAPS, PRESENTS
so fine a scope for bringing into full and constant play the
qualities both of the mind and body as that of Cricket. A man who
is essentially stupid will not make a fine cricketer ; neither will he
who is not essentially active. He must be active in all his faculties
—he must be active in mind to prepare for every advantage, and
active in eye and limb, to avail himself of those advantages. He
must be cool-tempered, and, in the best sense of the term, MANLY ;
for he must be able to endure fatigue, and to make light of pain ;
since, like all athletic sports, Cricket is not unattended with danger,
resulting from inattention or inexperience ; the accidents most
commonly attendant upon the players at cricket arising from
unwatchfulness, or slowness of eye. A short-sighted person is as
unfit to become a cricketer, as one deaf would be to discriminate
the most delicate gradations and varieties in tones ; added to
which, he must be in constant jeopardy of serious injury.

It is hoped that the present little work will be found a useful as
well as entertaining companion to the young practitioner in this
graceful and very exciting game. The name of NYREN was for many
years held in high estimation in the cricketing world ; he was the
father and general of the famous old Hambledon Club, which used
to hold its meetings on Broad-Halfpenny, and afterwards on
Windmill-down, near to Hambledon, in Hampshire. While old
Nyren directed their movements the Club remained unrivalled,
and frequently challenged all England. The most polished players
that this country ever produced were members of the Hambledon
Club—if John Nyren, the son of the good old patriarch, and father
of this little manual, be worthy of credit ; and many eminent
members of the Mary-le-bone Club, both " gentle and simple," can
attest his solid judgment, as well as his regard to truth and plain

dealing. Of the former class in society, the names of Lord Frederick Beauclerk, with Mr. Ward, and Mr. Ladbroke, will alone form ample testimony to his fitness to speak upon such points ; while his first-rate instruction, long practice, and superior accomplishment, will qualify him to impart his half a century's experience to the young practitioner.

The papers entitled "The Cricketers of My Time," which conclude the work, have already appeared in a weekly periodical. They have been collected at the desire of a few friends, and published here. If they afford any amusement to the young reader, it is to be wished that he may at the same time be led to emulate the skill of the most eminent men recorded in the different papers, and not wholly to disregard the sterling qualities of integrity, plain dealing, and good old English independence—the independence of native worth and moral rectitude, not of insolence and effrontery, which signalized many of their characters, and endeared them to their equals, while it commanded the respect of their superiors in rank and fortune.

All the players there recorded were either members or companions of the Hambledon Club, or their opponents. As it formed no part of Mr. Nyren's plan to include those of any other society, the reader will perceive why several players of recent date, equal, perhaps, in skill to those eminent veterans, have not been included. These may, possibly, be installed with their ancestors in some future edition of our little chronicle, if fate, and the Cricketers, decree in favour of a reprint.

C. C. C.

The Cricketers of my Time

THE GAME OF CRICKET IS THOROUGHLY BRITISH. ITS DERIVATION is probably from the Saxon " cpyce," a stick. Strutt, however, in his *Sports and Pastimes*, states that he can find no record of the game, under its present appellation, " beyond the commencement of the last century, where it occurs in one of the songs published by D'Urfey."[1] The first four lines of " Of a noble race was Shenkin," ran thus :—

> " Her was the prettiest fellow
> At foot-ball or at cricket,
> At hunting chase, or nimble race,
> How featly her could prick it."

The same historian of our games doubts not that cricket derived its origin from the ancient game of club-ball, the patronymics of which being compounded of Welch and Danish (clwppa and bol), do not warrant his conclusion, the Saxon being an elder occupant of our island. The circumstance, however, of there being no illustration extant—no missal, illuminated with a group engaged in this king of athletic games, as is the case with its plebeian brother, the club-ball ; also, from its constitution, being of a more civil and complicated character—we may rationally infer that it is the off-spring of a more polite, at all events, of a maturer age than its fellow. The game of club-ball appears to have been no other than the present well-known bat-and-ball, which, with similar laws and customs prescribed in the playing at it, was, doubtless, anterior to trap-ball. The trap, indeed carries with it an air of refinement in the "march of mechanism."

They who are acquainted with some of the remote and unfre-quented villages of England, where the primitive manners, customs, and games of our ancestors survive in the perfection of rude and

[1] " Pills to purge Melancholy," 4th edit. 1719, vol. ii. p. 172.

unadulterated simplicity must have remarked the lads playing at a
game which is the same in its outline and principal features as the
consummate piece of perfection that at this day is the glory of
Lord's and the pride of English athletæ—I mean the one in which
a single stick is appointed for a wicket, ditto for a bat, and the same
repeated, of about three inches in length, for a ball. If this be not
the original of the game of cricket, it is a plebeian imitation of it.

My purpose, however, is not to search into the antiquities of
cricketing, but to record my recollections of some of the most eminent
professors of my favourite pastime who have figured on the public
arena since the year 1776, when I might be about twelve years of age.
From that period till within a few seasons past, I have constantly been
" at the receipt of custom " when any rousing match has been
toward ; and being now a veteran, and laid up in ordinary, I may be
allowed the vanity of the quotation, " Quorum magna pars fui."[1]

I was born at Hambledon, in Hampshire—the Attica of the
scientific art I am celebrating. No eleven in England could compare
with the Hambledon, which met on the first Tuesday in May on
Broad-Halfpenny. So renowned a set were the men of Hambledon,
that the whole country round would flock to see one of their trial
matches. " Great men," indeed, " have been among us—better,
none " ; and in the course of my recollections I shall have occasion
to instance so many within the knowledge of persons now living, as
will, I doubt not, warrant me in giving the palm to my native place.

The two principal bowlers in my early days were THOMAS BRETT
and RICHARD NYREN of Hambledon ; the corps de reserve, or
change-bowlers, were BARBER and HOGSFLESH. Brett was, beyond
all comparison, the fastest as well as straightest bowler that was ever
known : he was neither a thrower nor a jerker, but a legitimate
downright bowler, delivering his ball fairly, high, and very quickly,
quite as strongly as the jerkers, and with the force of a point blank
shot. He was a well-grown, dark-looking man, remarkably strong,
and with rather a short arm. As a batter, he was comparatively an
inferior player—a slashing hitter, but he had little guard of his
wicket, and his judgment of the game was held in no great estimation.
Brett, whose occupation was that of a farmer, bore the universal
character of a strictly honourable man in all his transactions,
whether in business or in amusement.

---

[1] I learned a little Latin when I was a boy of a worthy old Jesuit, but I was a better
hand at the fiddle ; and many a time have I taught the gipseys a tune during their
annual visits to our village, thereby purchasing the security of our poultry-yard. When
the hand of the destroyer was stretched forth over the neighbouring roosts, our little
Goshen was always passed by.

Richard Nyren was left-handed. He had a high delivery, always to the length, and his balls were provokingly deceitful. He was the chosen General of all the matches, ordering and directing the whole. In such esteem did the brotherhood hold his experience and judgment, that he was uniformly consulted on all questions of law or precedent ; and I never knew an exception to be taken against his opinion, or his decision to be reversed. I never saw a finer specimen of the thorough-bred old English yeoman than Richard Nyren. He was a good face-to-face, unflinching, uncompromising, independent man. He placed a full and just value upon the station he held in society, and he maintained it without insolence or assumption. He could differ with a superior, without trenching upon his dignity, or losing his own. I have known him maintain an opinion with great firmness against the Duke of Dorset and Sir Horace Mann ; and when, in consequence, of his being proved to be in the right, the latter has afterwards crossed the ground and shaken him heartily by the hand. Nyren had immense advantage over Brett ; for, independently of his general knowledge of the game, he was practically a better cricketer, being a safe batsman and an excellent hitter. Although a very stout man (standing about five feet nine) he was uncommonly active. He owed all the skill and judgment he possessed to an old uncle, Richard Newland, of Slindon, in Sussex, under whom he was brought up—a man so famous in his time, that when a song was written in honour of the Sussex cricketers, Richard Newland was especially and honourably signalized. No one man ever dared to play him. When Richard Nyren left Hambledon, the club broke up, and never resumed from that day. The head and right arm were gone.

Barber and Hogsflesh were both good hands ; they had a high delivery, and a generally good length ; not very strong, however, at least for those days of playing when the bowling was all fast. These four were our tip-top men, and I think such another stud was not to be matched in the whole kingdom, either before or since. They were choice fellows, staunch and thorough-going. No thought of treachery ever seemed to have entered their heads. The modern politics of trickery and " crossing " were (so far as my own experience and judgment of their actions extended) as yet " a sealed book " to the Hambledonians ; what they did, they did for the love of honour and victory ; and when one (who shall be nameless) sold the birthright of his good name for a mess of potage, he paid dearly for his bargain. It cost him the trouble of being a knave— (no trifle !) ; the esteem of his old friends, and, what was worst of all, the respect of him who could have been his best friend—himself. Upon coming to the old batters of our club, the name of JOHN SMALL, the elder, shines among them in all the lustre of a star of the first magnitude. His merits have already been recorded in a separate publication, which every zealous brother of the pastime has probably read. I need, therefore, only subscribe my testimony to his uncommon talent, shortly summing up his chief excellencies. He was the best short runner of his day, and indeed I believe him to have been the first who turned the short hits to account. His decision was as prompt as his eye was accurate in calculating a short run. Add to the value of his accomplishment as a batter, he was an admirable field's-man, always playing middle wicket ; and so correct was his judgment of the game, that old Nyren would appeal to him when a point of law was being debated. Small was a remarkably well-made, and well-knit man, of honest expression, and as active as a hare.

He was a good fiddler, and taught himself the double bass. The Duke of Dorset having been informed of his musical talent, sent him as a present a handsome violin, and paid the carriage. Small, like a true and simple-hearted Englishman, returned the compliment, by sending his Grace two bats and balls, also paying the carriage. We may be sure that on both hands the presents were choice of their kind. Upon one occasion he turned his Orphean accomplishment to good account. Having to cross two or three fields on his way to a musical party, a vicious bull made at him ; when our hero, with the characteristic coolness and presence of mind of a good cricketer, began playing upon his bass, to the admiration and perfect satisfaction of the mischievous beast.

About this time, 1778, I became a sort of farmer's pony to my native club of Hambledon, and I never had cause to repent the work I was put to ; I gained by it that various knowledge of the game, which I leave in the hands of those who knew me in my " high and palmy state " to speak to and appreciate. This trifling preliminary being settled, the name and figure of TOM SUETER first comes across me—a Hambledon man, and of the club. What a handful of steel-hearted soldiers are in an important pass, such was Tom in keeping the wicket. Nothing went by him ; and for coolness, and nerve in this trying and responsible post, I never saw his equal. As a proof of his quickness and skill, I have numberless times seen him stump a man out with Brett's tremendous bowling. Add to this valuable accomplishment, he was one of the manliest and most graceful of hitters. Few would cut a ball harder at the point of the bat, and he was moreover, an excellent short runner. He had an eye like an eagle—rapid and comprehensive. He was the first who departed from the custom of the old players before him, who deemed it a heresy to leave the crease for the ball ; he would get in at it, and hit it straight off and straight on ; and, egad ! it went as if it had been fired. As by the rules of our club, at the trial-matches no man was allowed to get more than thirty runs, he generally gained his number earlier than any of them. I have seldom seen a handsomer man than Tom Sueter, who measured about five feet ten. As if, too, Dame Nature wished to show at his birth a specimen of her prodigality, she gave him so amiable a disposition, that he was the pet of all the neighbourhood : so honourable a heart, that his word was never questioned by the gentlemen who associated with him : and a voice, which for sweetness, power, and purity of tone (a tenor), would, with proper cultivation, have made him a handsome fortune. With what rapture have I hung upon his notes when he has given us a hunting song in the club room after the day's practice was over.

GEORGE LEAR, of Hambledon, who always answered to the title among us of " Little George," was our best long-stop. So firm and steady was he, that I have known him stand through a whole match against Brett's bowling, and not lose more than two runs. The ball seemed to go into him, and he was as sure of it as if he had been a sand bank. His activity was so great, and, besides, he had so good a judgment in running to cover the ball, that he would stop many that were hit in the slip, and this, be it remembered, from the swiftest bowling ever known. The portion of ground that man would cover was quite extraordinary. He was a good batsman, and a tolerably sure guard of his wicket ; he averaged from fifteen to twenty 1 ans, but I never remember his having a long innings. What he did not bring to the stock by his bat, however, he amply made up with his perfect fielding. Lear was a short man, of a fair complexion, well looking, and of a pleasing aspect. He had a sweet counter tenor voice. Many a treat have I had in hearing him and Sueter join in a glee at the " Bat and Ball " on Broad-Halfpenny :

> " I have been there, and still would go ;
> T'was like a little Heaven below ! "

EDWARD ABURROW, a native of Hambledon, was one of our best long fields. He always went by the name of Curry ; why, I cannot remember, neither is it of the utmost importance to enquire. He was well calculated for the post he always occupied, being a sure and strong thrower, and able to cover a great space of the field. He

was a steady and safe batter, averaging the same number of runs
as Lear. We reckoned him a tolerably good change for bowling.
Aburrow was a strong and well made man, standing about five feet
nine ; he had a plain, honest-looking face, and was beloved by all
his acquaintance.

BUCK, whose real name was PETER STEWARD, is the next Hambledon man that occurs to my recollection. He, too, played long
field, and was a steady man at his post ; his batting, too, reached
the same pitch of excellence ; he could cut the balls very hard at
the point of the bat—nothing like Sueter, however—very few could
have equalled him. Buck was a dark-looking man, a shoemaker by
trade, in height about five feet eight, rather slimly built, and very
active. He had an ambition to be thought a humourist. The
following anecdote may serve both as a specimen of his talent, and
of the unfastidious taste of the men of Hambledon. When a match
was to be played at a distance, the whole eleven, with the umpire
and scorer, were conveyed in one caravan, built for their accommo-
dation. Upon one occasion, the vehicle having been overturned,
and the whole cargo unshipped, Buck remained at his post, and
refused to come out, desiring that they would right the vessel with
him in it ; for that " one good turn deserved another." This
repartee was admired for a week.

The following old-fashioned song, and which was very popular
fifty years ago, may bring back pleasant recollections to those of my
countrymen who remember the Hambledon Club in the year 1778 :

CRICKET
BY THE REV. MR. COTTON, OF WINCHESTER.

Assist, all ye Muses, and join to rehearse
An old English sport, never praised yet in verse ;
'Tis Cricket I sing, of illustrious fame,
No nation e'er boasted so noble a game.
    Derry down, &c.

Great Pindar has bragg'd of his heroes of old—
Some were swift in the race, some in battles were bold ;
The brows of the victor with olives were crown'd :
Hark ! they shout, and Olympia returns the glad sound !
    Derry down, &c.

What boasting of Castor and Pollux's brother—
The one famed for riding, for boxing the other ;
Compared with our heroes, they'll not shine at all—

What were Castor and Pollux to Nyren and Small ?
    Derry down, &c.

Here's guarding and catching, and throwing and tossing,
And bowling and striking, and running and crossing ;
Each mate must excel in some principal part—
The Pentathlum of Greece could not show so much art.
    Derry down, &c.

The parties are met, and array'd all in white—
Famed Elis ne'er boasted so pleasing a sight ;
Each nymph looks askew at her favourite swain,
And views him, half stript, both with pleasure and pain,
    Derry down, &c.

The wickets are pitched now, and measured the ground ;
Then they form a large ring, and stand gazing around—
Since Ajax fought Hector, in sight of all Troy,
No contest was seen with such fear and such joy.
    Derry down, &c.

Ye bowlers, take heed, to my precepts attend :
On you the whole fate of the game must depend ;
Spare your vigour at first, now exert all your strength,
But measure each step, and be sure pitch a length ;
    Derry down, &c.

Ye fieldsmen, look sharp, lest your pains ye beguile ;
Move close like an army, in rank and in file ;
When the ball is returned, back it sure, for I trow,
Whole states have been ruined by one overthrow,
    Derry down, &c.

Ye strikers, observe when the foe shall draw nigh ;
Mark the bowler, advancing with vigilant eye ;
Your skill all depends upon distance and sight,
Stand firm to your scratch, let your bat be upright.
    Derry down, &c.

And now the game's o'er, IO victory ! rings,
Echo doubles her chorus, and Fame spreads her wings ;
Let's now hail our champions all steady and true,
Such as Homer ne'er sung of, nor Pindar e'er knew.
    Derry down, &c.

Buck, Curry, and Hogsflesh, and Barber and Brett,
Whose swiftness in bowling was ne'er equalled yet ;
I had almost forgot, they deserve a large bumper ;
Little George, the long stop, and Tom Sueter, the stumper.
 Derry down, &c.

Then why should we fear either Sackville or Mann,
Or repine at the loss both of Boynton and Lann ?—
With such troops as those we'll be lords of the game,
Spite of Minshull and Miller, and Lumpy and Frame.
 Derry down, &c.

Then fill up your glass, he's the best that drinks most.
Here's the Hambledon Club !—who refuses the toast ?
Lets join in the praise of the bat and the wicket,
And sing in full chorus the patrons of cricket.
 Derry down, &c.

And when the game's o'er, and our fate shall draw nigh,
(For the heroes of cricket, like others, must die,)
Our bats we'll resign, neither troubled nor vex'd,
And give up our wickets to those that come next.
 Derry down, &c.

The tenth knight of our round table (of which old Richard Nyren
was the King Arthur), was a man we always called " The Little
Farmer " ; his name was LAMBERT. He was a bowler—right-
handed, and he had the most extraordinary delivery I ever saw.
The ball was delivered quite low, and with a twist ; not like that
of the generality of right-handed bowlers, but just the reverse way :
that is, if bowling to a right-handed hitter, his ball would twist from
the off stump into the leg. He was the first I remember who introduced this deceitful and teasing style of delivering the ball. When
all England played the Hambledon Club, the Little Farmer was
appointed one of our bowlers ; and, egad ! this new trick of his so
bothered the Kent and Surrey men, that they tumbled out one
after another, as if they had been picked off by a rifle corps. For
a long time they could not tell what to make of that cursed twist of
his. This, however, was the only virtue he possessed, as a cricketer.
He was no batter, and had no judgment of the game. The perfection
he had attained in this one department, and his otherwise general
deficiency, are at once accounted for by the circumstance, that when
he was tending his father's sheep, he would set up a hurdle or two,
and bowl away for hours together. Our General, old Nyren, after

a great deal of trouble (for the Farmer's comprehension did not equal the speed of lightning), got him to pitch the ball a little to the off-side of the wicket, when it twist full in upon the stumps. Before he had got into this knack, he was once bowling against the Duke of Dorset, and, delivering his ball straight to the wicket, it curled in, and missed the Duke's leg-stump by a hair's breadth. The plain-spoken little bumpkin, in his eagerness and delight, and forgetting the style in which we were always accustomed to impress our aristocratical playmates with our acknowledgment of their rank and station, bawled out—" Ah ! it was *tedious* near you, Sir ! " The familiarity of his tone, and the genuine Hampshire dialect in which it was spoken, set the whole ground laughing. I have never seen but one bowler who delivered his balls in the same way as our Little Farmer ; with the jerkers the practice is not uncommon. He was a very civil and inoffensive young fellow, and remained in the club perhaps two or three seasons.

With Tom Taylor the old eleven was completed. There were, of course, several changes of other players, but these were the established picket set—the elite. Tom was an admirable field— certainly one of the very finest I ever saw. His station was between the point of the bat and the middle wicket, to save the two runs ; but Tom had a lucky knack of gathering in to the wicket, for Tom had a license from our old General ; so that, if the ball was hit to him, he had so quick a way of meeting it, and with such a rapid return (for no sooner was it in his hand than with the quickness of thought it was returned to the top of the wicket) that I have seen many put out by this manœuvre in a single run, and when the hit might be safely calculated upon for a prosperous one. He had an excellent general knowledge of the game ; but of fielding, in particular, he was perfect both in judgment and practice. Tom was also a most brilliant hitter, but his great fault lay in not suffi-ciently guarding his wicket : he was too fond of cutting, at the point of the bat, balls that were delivered straight ; although, therefore, he would frequently get many runs, yet, from this habit, he could not be securely depended on ; and, indeed, it was commonly the cause of his being out. I have known Lord Frederick Beauclerk (certainly the finest batter of his day) throw away the chance of a capital innings by the same incaution—that of cutting at straight balls, and he has been bowled out in consequence. Taylor was a short, well made man, strong, and as watchful and active as a cat ; but in no other instance will the comparison hold good, for he was without guile, and was an attached friend.

Having now described the best of my native players, I proceed to their opponents ; and the foremost man of all, must stand the well-known bowler, LUMPY, whose real name was STEVENS. He was a Surrey man, and lived with Lord Tankerville. Beyond all the men within my recollection Lumpy would bowl the greatest number of length balls in succession. His pace was much faster than Lord Beauclerk's, but he wanted his Lordship's general knowledge of the game. In those days it was the custom for the party going from home to pitch their own wickets ; and here it was that Lumpy, whose duty it was to attend to this, always committed an error. He would invariably choose the ground where his balls would *shoot*, instead of selecting a rising spot to bowl against, which would have materially increased the difficulty to the hitter, seeing that so many more would be caught out by the mounting of the ball. As nothing, however, delighted the old man like bowling a wicket down with a shooting ball, he would sacrifice the other chances to the glory of that achievement. Many a time have I seen our General twig this prejudice in the old man when matched against us, and chuckle at it. But I believe it was almost the only mistake he ever made professional, or even moral, for he was a most simple and amiable creature. Yes—one other he committed, and many a day after was the joke remembered against him. One of our matches having been concluded early in the day, a long, rawboned devil of a countryman came up, and offered to play any one of the twenty-two at single wicket for five pounds. Old Nyren told Lumpy it would be five pounds easily earned, and persuaded him to accept the challenge. Lumpy however, would not stake the whole sum himself, but offered a pound of the money, the rest was subscribed. The confident old bowler made the countryman go in first, for he thought to settle his business in a twink : but the fellow having an arm as long as a hop-pole, reached in at Lumpy's balls, bowl what length he might ; and slashed and thrashed away in the most ludicrous style, hitting his balls all over the field and always up in the air ; and he made an uncommon number of runs from this prince of bowlers before he could get him out ; and, egad ! he beat him !—for when Lumpy went in, not being a good batter, while the other was a very fast bowler, all along the ground, and straight to the wicket, he knocked him out presently ; the whole ring roaring with laughter, and the astounded old bowler swearing he would never play another single match as long as he lived—an oath, I am sure, he religiously observed, for he was confoundedly crest-fallen. Lumpy was a short man, round-shouldered, and stout. He had no trick about him, but was as plain as a pike-staff in all his dealings.

FRAME was the other principal with Lumpy ; a fast bowler, and an unusually stout man for a cricketer. I recollect very little of him, and nothing worthy of a formal record.

Besides him there was SHOCK WHITE, another bowler on the England side ; a good change, and a very decent hitter ; but take him altogether, I never thought very highly of his playing. He was a short and rather stoutly made man.

JOHN WOOD made the fourth, and the other change bowler. He was tall, stout, and bony, and a very good general player ; not, however, an extraordinary one, when compared with those that have been heretofore mentioned.

There was high feasting held on Broad-Halfpenny during the solemnity of one of our grand matches. Oh ! it was a heart-stirring sight to witness the multitude forming a complete and dense circle round that noble green. Half the county would be present, and all their hearts with us. Little Hambledon, pitted against all England, was a proud thought for the Hampshire man. Defeat was glory in such a struggle—victory, indeed, made us only " a little lower than angels." How those fine brawn-faced fellows of farmers would drink to our success ! And then, what stuff they had to drink !— Punch !—not your new *Ponche a la Romaine,* or *Ponche a la Grosielle,* or your modern cat-lap milk punch—punch be-deviled ; but good, unsophisticated, John Bull stuff—stark !—that would stand on end—punch that would make a cat speak ! Sixpence a bottle. We had not sixty millions of interest to pay in those days. The ale, too !—not the modern horror under the same name, that drives as many men melancholy-mad as the hypocrites do ;—not the beastliness of these days, that will make a fellow's inside like a shaking bog—and as rotten ; but barley-corn, such as would put the souls of three butchers into one weaver. Ale that would flare like turpentine—genuine Boniface ! This immortal viand (for it was more than liquor) was vended at twopence per pint. The immeasurable villiany of our vintners would, with their march of intellect (if ever they could get such a brewing), drive a pint of it out into a gallon. Then the quantity the fellows would eat ! Two or three of them would strike dismay into a round of beef. They could no more have pecked in that style than they could have flown, had the infernal black stream (that type of Acheron !) which soddens the carcass of a Londoner, been the fertilizer of their clay. There would this company, consisting most likely of some thousands, remain patiently and anxiously watching every turn of fate in the game, as if the event had been the meeting of two armies to decide their liberty. And whenever a Hambledon man made a good hit, worth four or five runs, you would hear the deep mouths of the whole multitude baying away in pure Hampshire—" Go hard ! go hard !—*Tich* and turn !—*tich* and turn ! " To the honour of my countrymen, let me bear testimony upon this occasion also, as I have already done upon others. Although their provinciality in general, and personal partialities individually, were naturally interested in behalf of the Hambledon men, I cannot call to recollection an instance of their wilfully stopping a ball that had been hit out among them by one of our opponents. Like *true* Englishmen, they would give an enemy fair play. How strongly are all those scenes, of fifty years by-gone, painted in my memory !—and the smell of that ale comes upon me as freshly as the new May flowers.

Having premised that these grand matches were always made for 500 *l*. aside, I now proceed with a slight record of the principal men who were usually pitted against us. My description of them must unavoidably be less minute, because I had not so frequent an intercourse with them as with the men whose every action I was constantly in the habit of watching : my report of them, therefore, may be more slight than their merits deserve, for there were really some fine players among them. For the same reason also, my chronicle will be less relieved by personal anecdote.

My last account having closed with the four principal bowlers who were usually opposed to us—Lumpy and Frame, Shock White and Wood—the next name that presents itself to me is that of MINSHULL, who was a gardener to the Duke of Dorset. He was a batter, and a very fine one—probably their best ; a capital hitter, and a sure guard of his wicket. Minshull, however, was not an elegant player ; his position and general style were both awkward and uncouth ; yet he was as conceited as a wagtail, and from his constantly aping what he had no pretensions to, was, on that account only, not estimated according to the price at which he had rated his own merits. He was a thick-set man, standing about five feet nine, and not very active.

MILLER (game-keeper either to Lord Tankerville or the Duke of Dorset, I forget which) was as amiable a hearted man as ever cut a ball at the point of the bat. He and Minshull were the only two batters the Hambledon men were afraid of. Miller was indeed a beautiful player, and always to be depended on ; there was no flash—no cock-a-whoop about him, but firm he was, and steady as the pyramids. Although fully as stout a man as Minshull, he was considerably more active. I remember when on one occasion those two men, being in together, had gained an uncommon number of runs, the backers of the Hambledon men, Dehaney and Paulet, began to quake, and edged off all their money, laying it pretty thickly on the England side. Of the Hambledon men, Small went in first, and continued until there were about five out, for very few runs, when Nyren went in to him ; and then they began to show fight. The mettle of our true blood was roused into full action, and never did they exhibit to finer advantage. Nyren got 98, and Small 110 runs before they were parted. After the former was out (for Small, according to his custom, died a natural death) the backers came up to Nyren and said, " You will win the match, and we shall lose our money." The proud old yeoman turned short upon them, and, with that honest independence which gained him the esteem of all parties, told them to their heads that they were rightly served, and that he was glad of it. " Another time (said he) don't bet your money against such men as we are ! " I forget how many runs the Hambledon met got, but, after this turn in affairs, the others stood no chance, and were easily beaten.

MAY and BOOKER, and QUIDDINGTON, were players of the first rank, though not the first of that rank. They were excellent and steady batters, strong hitters, and sure fields. Quiddington was a long-stop, and an admirable one ; not, however, so implicitly to be depended on as Lear, whose equal in that department of the game I never saw any where. My reason for assigning him this superiority has been already given. For the same cause, too, I must place our Sueter above Yalden, who was their best wicket keeper, and he would have been highly prized anywhere ; but neither he nor Quiddington ever had to stand against such steam-engine bowling as Brett's ; and yet Lear and Sueter, in their several departments, were safer men than their opponents. Yalden, too, was in other respects an inferior man to Sueter. His word was not always to be depended on when he had put a man out—he would now and then shuffle and resort to trick. In such estimation did the other stand with all parties so high an opinion had they of his honour—that I firmly believe they would have trusted to his decision, had he ever chosen to question that of the umpire. Yalden was not a fine, but a very useful and steady batter. He was a thin, dark-looking man.

The DUKE OF DORSET, or LORD TANKERVILLE, sometimes both, would play, to complete the eleven. Neither of these noblemen were to be compared to Lord Frederick Beauclerk. Whether in batting, bowling, or indeed in any department of the game, he would have distanced them ; yet they were pretty players. Each usually played in the slip when the other was not present. This station was the Duke's *forte*. He was in height about five feet nine, very well made, and had a peculiar habit, when unemployed, of standing with his head on one side.

About the period I have been describing, NOAH MANN joined the Hambledon Club. He was from Sussex, and lived at North Chapel, not far from Petworth. He kept an inn there, and used to come a distance of at least twenty miles every Tuesday to practice. He was a fellow of extraordinary activity, and could perform clever feats of agility on horseback. For instance, when he has been seen in the distance coming up the ground, one or more of his companions would throw down handkerchiefs, and these he would collect, stooping from his horse while it was going at full speed. He was a fine batter, a fine field, and the swiftest runner I ever remember ; indeed, such was his fame for speed, that whenever there was a match going forward, we were sure to hear of one being made for Mann to run against some noted competitor ; and such would come from the whole country round. Upon these occasions he used to tell his friends, " If, when we are half-way, you see me alongside of my man, you may always bet your money upon me, for I am sure to win." And I never saw him beaten. He was a most valuable fellow in the field ; for besides being very sure of the ball, his activity was so extraordinary that he would dart all over the ground like lightning. In those days of fast bowling, they would put a man behind the long-stop, that he might cover both long stop and slip : the man always selected for this post was Noah. Now and then little George Lear (whom I have already described as being so fine a long-stop), would give Noah the wink to be on his guard, who would gather close behind him : then George would make a slip on purpose, and let the ball go by, when, in an instant, Noah would have it up, and into the wicket keeper's hands, and the man was put out. This I have seen done many times, and this nothing but the most accomplished skill in fielding could have achieved.

Mann would, upon occasion, be employed as a change-bowler, and in this department he was very extraordinary. He was left-handed, both as bowler and batter. In the former quality, his merit consisted in giving a curve to the ball the whole way. In itself it was not the first-rate style of bowling, but so very deceptive, that the chief end was frequently attained. They who remember the dexterous manner with which the Indian jugglers communicated the curve to the balls they spun round their heads, by a twist of the wrist or hand, will at once comprehend Noah's curious feat in bowling. Sometimes when a batter had got into his hitting, and was scoring more runs than pleased our General, he would put Mann in to give him eight or twelve balls, and he almost always did so with good effect.

Noah was a good batsman, and a most severe hitter ; by the way, I have observed this to be a common quality in left-handed men. The writer of this was in with him at a match on Windmill-down, when, by one stroke from a toss that he hit behind him we got ten runs. At this time the playing-ground was changed from Board-Halfpenny to the above named spot, at the suggestion of the Duke of Dorset and the other gentlemen, who complained of the bleakness of the old place. The alteration was in this, as in every other respect, for the better, Windmill-down being one of the finest places for playing on I ever saw. The ground gradually declined every way from the centre : the fieldsmen therefore were compelled to look about them, and for this reason they became so renowned in that department of the game.

At a match of the Hambledon Club against all England, the club had to go in to get the runs, and there was a long number of them. It became quite apparent that the game would be closely fought. Mann kept on worrying Old Nyren to let him go in, and although he became quite indignant at his constant refusal, our General knew what he was about in keeping him back. At length, when the last but one was out, he sent Mann in, and there were then ten runs to get. The sensation now all over the ground was greater than anything of the kind I ever witnessed before or since. All knew the state of the game, and many thousands were hanging upon this narrow point. There was Sir Horace Mann, walking about, outside the ground, cutting down the daisies with his stick— a habit with him when he was agitated ; the old farmers leaning forward upon their tall old staves, and the whole multitude perfectly still. After Noah had had one or two balls, Lumpy tossed one a little too far, when our fellow got in, and hit it out in his grand style. Six of the ten were gained. Never shall I forget the roar that followed this hit. Then there was a dead stand for some time, and no runs were made ; ultimately, however, he gained them all, and won the game. After he was out, he upbraided Nyren for not putting him in earlier. " If you had let me go in an hour ago (said he), I would have served them in the same way." But the old tactician was right, for he knew Noah to be a man of such nerve and self-possession, that the thought of so much depending upon him, would not have the paralyzing effect that it would upon many others. He was sure of him ; and Noah afterwards felt the compliment. Mann was short in stature, and, when stripped, as swarthy as a gipsy. He was all muscle, with no incumbrance whatever of flesh ; remarkably broad in the chest, with large hips and spider legs : he had not an ounce of flesh about him, but it was where it ought to be. He always played without his hat (the sun could not affect *his* complexion), and he took a liking to me as a boy, because I did the same. Poor Noah ! his death was a very deplorable one. Having been out shooting all day with some friends, they finished their evening with a free carouse, and he could not be persuaded to go to bed, but persisted in sleeping all night in his chair in the chimney corner. It was, and still is, the custom in that part of the country, to heap together all the ashes on the hearth, for the purpose of keeping the fire in till the next day. During the night my poor playmate fell upon the embers, and being unable to help himself, burned his side so severely, that he did not survive twenty-four hours.

RICHARD FRANCIS was a Surrey man. One day I met him in the street of Hambledon, and ran to tell our General that the famous Francis had come to live amongst us ; he could scarcely believe me —perhaps for joy. This was the luckiest thing that could have happened for us, for Brett had just about the same time left off playing. Francis was a fast *jerker* ; but though his delivery was allowed to be fair bowling, still it was a jerk. We enlisted him immediately, for we all knew what he could do, having seen him play on the Surrey side against us. At that time he was a young man, and he remained many years in the club. He was a game-keeper ; a closely made, firm little man, and active. His batting did not deserve any marked praise, still we always set him down for a few runs. He was both a better batter, however, and field too, than Brett ; but as a bowler, he ranked many degrees below that fine player.

About the same period RICHARD PURCHASE joined us. He was a slowish bowler—rather faster than Lord Beauclerk. His balls got up uncommonly well, and they were generally to a length. But he had no cunning about him ; nor was he up to the tricks of the game. In playing, as in all other actions in life, he was the same straight-forward honest fellow. Purchase was a fair hitter, and a tolerably good field. He was a slightly made man, and of a dark complexion

At this great distance from the period at which my recollection of cricketing commenced, and having no data by which to regulate them, the reader will good-naturedly make allowance both for the desultory character of my records, their unfinished and hasty sketchiness, and also for my now and then retracing my steps, to include some circumstance which, at the time of writing, had escaped my memory. For instance, I should have chronicled the era when the old-fashioned wicket of *two* stumps was changed to *three*—a decided improvement, seeing that it multiplied the chances to the batter of being bowled out, consequently increased the diffi-culties of his position, and thereby exalted his maintaining it for any length of time into the greater merit ; for, under the old system, if the ball passed between the stumps, the batter was not considered out ; under the improved system, such an event cannot happen, for the three stumps are not pitched at so great a distance from each other as to allow of the transit of the ball without knocking off the bail. This explanation is, of course, addressed only to the young and inexperienced player. The important reform in the game here alluded to took place, according to the best of my recollection, about the year 1779 or 1780. Since that time other entrenchments have been made upon the old constitution, which was the pride of our ancestors and the admiration of the whole community ; but which, so far from contributing to its stability, will, in my opinion, if not retrieved, not only essentially change, but even destroy its character ; let the patrician legislators and guardians of cricket-law look to it.

Before I proceed with my catalogue of the Hambledon Pantheon, it may be worth while to mention a circumstance connected with poor Noah Mann, the player named a few pages back. As it will tend to show the amenity in which the men of lower grade in society lived in those good old times with their superiors, it may prove no worthless example to the more aristocratic, and certainly less beloved members of the same rank in society of the present day. Poor Noah was very ambitious that his new-born son should bear the christian name, with the sanction of his namesake, Sir Horace Mann. Old Nyren, who, being the link between the patricians and plebeians in our community—the *juste milieu*—was always applied to in cases of similar emergency, undertook, upon the present occasion, to bear the petition of Noah to Sir Horace, who, with a winning condescension, acceded to the worthy fellow's request, and consented to become godfather to the child, giving it his own name ; adding, I have no doubt, a present suited to the station of his little protege. How easy a thing it is to win the esteem of our inferiors ;

and how well worth the while, when the mutual pleasure only, resulting from the action, is considered ! Sir Horace, by this simple act of graceful humanity, hooked for life the heart of poor Noah Mann ; and in this world of hatred and contention, the love even of a dòg is worth living for.

The next player I shall name is JAMES AYLWARD. His father was a farmer. After he had played with the club for a few years, Sir Horace got him away from us, and made him his bailiff, I think, or some such office ; I remember, however, he was but ill-qualified for his post. Aylward was a left-handed batter, and one of the safest hitters I ever knew in the club. He once staid in two whole days, and upon that occasion got the highest number of runs that had ever been gained by any member—*one hundred and sixty-seven !* Jemmy was not a good fieldsman, neither was he remarkably active. After he left us, to go down to live with Sir Horace, he played against us, but never to my recollection with any advantage to his new associates—the Hambledonians were almost always too strong for their opponents. He was introduced to the club by Tom Taylor, and Tom's anxiety upon the occasion, that his friend should do credit to his recommendation, was curiously conspicuous. Aylward was a stout, well-made man, standing about five feet nine inches ; not very light about the limbs, indeed he was rather clumsy. He would sometimes affect a little grandeur of manner, and once got laughed at by the whole ground for calling for a lemon to be brought to him when he had been in but a little while. It was thought a piece of finickiness by those simple and homely yeomen.

And now for those anointed clod-stumpers, the WALKERS, TOM and HARRY. Never sure came two such unadulterated rustics into a civilized community. How strongly are the figures of the men (of Tom's in particular) brought to my mind when they first presented themselves to the club, upon Windmill-down. Tom's hard, ungain, scrag-of-mutton frame ; wilted, apple-john face (he always looked twenty years older than he really was), his long spider legs, as thick at the ankles as at the hips, and perfectly straight all the way down—for the embellishment of a calf in Tom's leg, Dame Nature had considered would be but a wanton superfluity. Tom was the driest and most rigid-limbed chap I ever knew ; his skin was like the rind of an old oak, and as sapless. I have seen his knuckles handsomely knocked about from Harris's bowling ; but never saw any blood upon his hands—you might just as well attempt to phlebotomize a mummy. This rigidity of muscle (or rather I should say of tendon, for muscle was another ingredient economized in the process of Tom's configuration)—this rigidity, I say, was carried into every motion. He moved like the rude machinery of a steam-engine in the infancy of construction, and when he ran, every member seemed ready to fly to the four winds. He toiled like a tar on horseback. The uncouth actions of these men furnished us, who prided ourselves upon a certain grace in movement and finished air, with an everlasting fund of amusement, and for some time they took no great fancy to me, because I used to worry, and tell them they could not play. They were, however, good hands when they first came among us, and had evidently received most excellent instruction ; but after they had derived the advantage of first-rate practice, they became most admirable batters, and were the trustiest fellows (particularly Tom) in cases of emergency or difficulty. They were devilish troublesome customers to get out. I have very frequently known Tom to go in first, and remain to the very last man. He was the coolest, the most imperturbable fellow in existence ; it used to be said of him that he had no nerves at all. Whether he was only practising, or whether he knew that the game was in a critical state, and that much depended upon his play, he was the same phlegmatic, unmoved man—he was the Washington of cricketers. Neither he nor his brother were active, yet both were effective fieldsmen. Upon one occasion, on the Mary-le-bone grounds, I remember Tom going in first, and Lord Beauclerk giving him the first four balls, all of an excellent length. First four or last four made no difference to Tom—he was always the same cool, collected fellow. Every ball he dropped down just before his bat. Off went his lordship's white hat—dash upon the ground (his constant action when disappointed), calling him at the same time " a confounded old beast." " I doant care what ee zays," said Tom, when one close by asked if he had heard Lord Frederick call him " an old beast." No, no ; Tom was not the man to be flustered.

About a couple of years after Walker had been with us, he began the system of throwing instead of bowling, now so much the fashion. At that time, it was esteemed foul play, and so it was decided by a council of the Hambledon Club, which was called for the purpose. The first I recollect seeing revive the custom was Wills, a Sussex man. I am decidedly of the opinion, that if it be not stopped altogether, the character of the game will become changed. I should hope that such powerful and efficient members of the Mary-le-bone Club, as Mr. Ward, etc., will determine, not only to discountenance, but wholly and finally to suppress it ; and instead, to foster and give every encouragement to genuine, bona fide bowlers—men with a fine delivery.

I never thought much of Tom's bowling ; indeed the bowling of that time was so supereminent, that he was not looked upon as a bowler—even for a change. He afterwards, however, greatly improved ; and what with his thorough knowledge of the game, his crafty manner (for he was one of the most fox-headed fellows I ever saw), and his quickness in seizing every advantage, he was of considerable service to his party, but he never was a first-rate bowler. He was a right, and Harry a left-handed batter, and both were valuable men. They came from Thursley, near Hindhead ; they and their father were farmers, and their land lay near to the Devil's punch-bowl.

The next in succession will be JOHN WELLS, the BELDHAMS, HARRIS, and FREEMANTLE.

Shortly after the Walkers had joined us, JOHN WELLS became a member of the Hambledon Club. John lived at Farnham, in Surrey, and was, if I recollect, a baker by trade. He was a short, thick, well-set man ; in make like a cob-horse, proportionately strong, active and laborious. As a bowler, he had a very good delivery ; he was also a good general field, and a steady batter—in short, an excellent " servant of all work " ; and, like those misused Gibeonites (" hewers of wood and drawers of water,") he was never spared when a wear-and-tear post was to be occupied. In cricket, as in the graver pursuits in life, the willing workman is ever spurred ; he may perform labours of supererogation, and his assiduity meets at best with " mouth honour " : let him, however, but relax his muscles—let him but shorten his career to the speed of his fellows, and he instantly sinks below them in the estimation of his employers. Whether in this case, the feeling arise from envy or not, it is hard to decide ; assuredly, however, in very many instances, the mill-horse-grinder in the track of duty is acknowledged with greeting, while extra merit " goes out sighing." John Wells possessed all the requisites for making a thoroughly useful cricketer ; and in his general deportment, he was endowed with those qualities which render man useful to society as well as happy in himself. He was a creature of a transparent and unflawed integrity—plain, simple, and candid ; uncompromising, yet courteous ; civil and deferential, yet no cringer. He always went by the title of " Honest John Wells," and as long as I knew him, he never forfeited the character he had gained. Little more need be added respecting his merits as a player, for he must be fresh in the memory of all who have been accustomed to see the best playing ; suffice to say, that in addition to his level merits as a general cricketer, he was esteemed to possess an excellent judgment of the game, and in questions that were frequently mooted, his opinion would be appealed to. The BELDHAMS, GEORGE and WILLIAM, come next in succession, brothers, and both farmers. They also, with Wells, came from Farnham. George was what would be called a fine player ; a good batter, and generally competent to fill the different posts in the game ; but as he attended the club a few times only during my stay in it, I am unable to discriminate or speak pointedly to his merits. Upon turning, however, to his brother William, we come to the finest batter of his own, or perhaps of any age. William Beldham was a close-set, active man, standing about five feet eight inches and a half. He had light-coloured hair, a fair complexion, and handsome as well as intelligent features. We used to call him " Silver Billy." No one within my recollection could stop a ball better, or make more brilliant hits all over the ground. Wherever the ball was bowled, there she was hit away, and in the most severe, venomous style. Besides this, he was so remarkably safe a player ; he was safer than the Bank, for no mortal ever thought of doubting Beldham's stability. He received his instructions from a gingerbread baker at Farnham, of the name of Harry Hall. I once played against Hall, and found him a very fair hand, yet nothing remarkable ; he knew the principles of the game, yet, like many of inferior merit in performance, he made nevertheless an excellent tutor. He was a slow bowler, and a pretty good one. He had a peculiar habit of bringing his hand from behind his back immediately previous to his delivering the ball, a trick no doubt perplexing enough to an inexperienced batter. In his peripatetic lectures to the young students, Hall perpetually enforced the principle of keeping the *left* elbow well up (this charge was of course delivered to the *right*-handed hitters), and excellent instruction it was ; for if you do keep that elbow well up, and your bat also upright (in stopping a *length ball*), you will not fail to keep the balls down ; and, *vice versa*, lower your elbow, and your balls will infallibly mount when you strike them.

BELDHAM was quite a young man when he joined the Hambledon Club ; and even in that stage of his playing, I hardly ever saw a man with a finer command of his bat ; but, with the instruction and advice of the old heads superadded, he rapidly attained to the extraordinary accomplishment of being the finest player that has appeared within the latitude of more than half a century. There can be no exception against his batting, or the severity of his hitting.

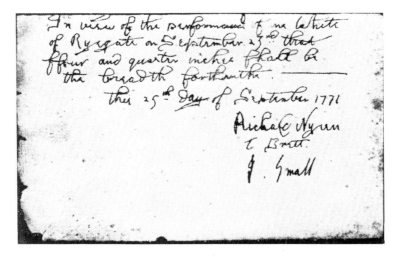

Figure 2. A minute of the Hambledon players, 1771, which limited the width of the bat to 4¼″ after 'Shock' White of Reigate had attempted to use a bat as wide as the wicket.

Figure 3. John Frederick Sackville, 3rd Duke of Dorset, player and patron, whose last recorded match was against the Hambledon Club in 1783.

David Harris

Walter Beldam

Figure 4. David Harris (top) the Hambledon Club's greatest bowler, and William Beldham 'the very best batter'. From drawings by George Shepheard, ca. 1790.

He would get in at the balls, and hit them away in a gallant style ;
yet, in this single feat, I think I have known him excelled ; but
when he could cut them at the point of his bat, he was in his glory ;
and upon my life, their speed was as the speed of thought. One of
the most beautiful sights that can be imagined, and which would
have delighted an artist, was to see him make himself up to hit a
ball. It was the beau ideal of grace, animation, and concentrated
energy. In this peculiar exhibition of elegance with vigour, the
nearest approach to him I think was Lord Frederick Beauclerk.
Upon one occasion at Mary-le-bone, I remember these two admirable batters being in together, and though Beldham was then
verging towards his climacteric, yet both were excited to a competition, and the display of talent that was exhibited between them
that day was the most interesting sight of its kind I ever witnessed.
I should not forget, among his other excellencies, to mention that
Beldham was one of the best judges of a short run I ever knew, add
to which, that he possessed a generally good knowledge of the game.

Hitherto I have spoken only of his batting. In this department
alone, he had talent enough to make a dozen ordinary cricketers,
but as a general fieldsman there were few better ; he could take
any post in the field, and do himself credit in it : latterly he usually
chose the place of slip. But Beldham was a good change bowler,
too ; he delivered his balls high, and they got up well. His pace
was a moderate one, yet bordering upon the quick. His principal
fault in this department was, that he would often give a toss ; taking
him however, as a change bowler, he was one of the best. He would
very quickly discover what a hitter could do, and what he could
not do, and arrange his bowling accordingly. Finally, although
his balls were commonly to the length, he was much better calculated for a change than to be continued a considerable length of time.

One of the finest treats in cricketing that I remember, was to
see this admirable man in, with the beautiful bowling of Harris.

Having finished with the best batter of his own, or, perhaps, of
any age—Beldham, we proceed to the very best bowler ; a bowler
who, between any one and himself, comparison must fail. DAVID
HARRIS was, I believe, born, at all events he lived at Odiham, in
Hampshire ; he was by trade a potter. He was a muscular, bony
man, standing about five feet nine and a half inches. His features
were not regularly handsome, but a remarkably kind and gentle
expression amply compensated the defect of mere linear beauty.
The fair qualities of his heart shone through his honest face, and I
can call to mind no worthier, or, in the active sense of the word, not

a more " *good* man " than David Harris. He was one of the rare
species that link man to man in bonds of fellowship by good works ;
that inspire confidence, and prevent the structure of society from
becoming disjointed, and, " as it were, a bowing wall, or a tottering
fence." He was a man of so strict a principle, and such high honour,
that I believe his moral character was never impeached. I never
heard even a suspicion breathed against his integrity, and I knew
him long and intimately. I do not mean that he was a *canter*.
Oh, no—no one thought of standing on guard, and buttoning up
his pockets in Harris's company. I never busied myself about his
mode of faith, or the peculiarity of his creed ; that was his own
affair, not mine, or any other being's on earth ; all I know is, that
he was an " honest man," and the poet has assigned the rank of
such a one in creation.

It would be difficult, perhaps impossible, to convey in writing
an accurate idea of the grand effect of Harris's bowling ; they only
who have played against him can fully appreciate it. His attitude
when preparing for his run previously to delivering the ball, would
have made a beautiful study for the sculptor. Phidias would certainly have taken him for a model. First of all, he stood erect like
a soldier at drill ; then, with a graceful curve of the arm, he raised
the ball to his forehead, and drawing back his right foot, started
off with his left. The calm look and general air of the man were
uncommonly striking, and from this series of preparations he never
deviated. I am sure that from this simple account of his manner,
all my countrymen who were acquainted with his play will recall
him to their minds. His mode of delivering the ball was very
singular. He would bring it from under the arm by a twist, and
nearly as high as his arm-pit, and with this action *push* it, as it were,
from him. How it was that the balls acquired the velocity they
did by this mode of delivery I never could comprehend.

When first he joined the Hambledon Club, he was quite a raw
countryman at cricket, and had very little to recommend him but
his noble delivery. He was also very apt to give tosses. I have seen
old Nyren scratch his head, and say—" Harris would make the best
bowler in England if he did not toss." By continual practice,
however, and following the advice of the old Hambledon players,
he became as steady as could be wished ; and in the prime of his
playing very rarely indeed gave a toss, although his balls were
pitched the full length. In bowling, he never stooped in the least
in his delivery, but kept himself upright all the time. His balls were
very little beholden to the ground when pitched ; it was but a

touch, and up again ; and woe be to the man who did not get in to block them, for they had such a peculiar curl that they would grind his fingers against the bat ; many a time have I seen the blood drawn in this way from a batter who was not up to the trick : old Tom Walker was the only exception—I have before classed him among the bloodless animals.

Harris's bowling was the finest of all tests for a hitter, and hence the great beauty, as I observed before of seeing Beldham in, with this man against him ; for unless a batter were of the very first class, and accustomed to the best style of stopping, he could do little or nothing with Harris. If the thing had been possible, I should have liked to have seen such a player as Budd (fine hitter as he was) standing against him. My own opinion is, that he could not have stopped his balls, and this will be a criterion, by which those who have seen some of that gentleman's brilliant hits, may judge of the extraordinary merit of this man's bowling. He was considerably faster than Lambert, and so superior in style and finish, that I can draw no comparison between them. Lord Frederick Beauclerk has been heard to say that Harris's bowling was one of the grandest things of the kind he had ever seen ; but his Lordship could not have known him in his prime ; he never saw him play until after he had had many fits of the gout, and had become slow and feeble.

To Harris's fine bowling I attribute the great improvement that was made in hitting, and above all in stopping ; for it was utterly impossible to remain at the crease, when the ball was tossed to a fine length ; you were obliged to get in, or it would be about your hands, or the handle of your bat ; and every player knows where its next place would be.

Some years after Harris had played with the Hambledon Club, he became so well acquainted with the science of the game of cricket, that he could take a very great advantage in pitching the wickets. And not only would he pitch a good wicket for himself, but he would also consider those who had to bowl with him. The writer of this has often walked with him up to Windmill-down at six o'clock in the morning of the day that a match was to be played, and has with pleasure noticed the pains he has taken in choosing the ground for his fellow-bowler as well as himself. The most eminent men in every walk of life have at all times been the most painstaking ; slabberdash work and indifference may accompany genius, and it does so too frequently ; such geniuses, however, throw away more than half their chance. There are more brilliant talents in this world than people give the world credit for ; and that their lustre does not exhibit to the best advantage, commonly depends upon the owners of them.   Ill luck, and the preference that frequently attends industrious mediocrity, are the only anodynes that wounded self-love or indolence can administer to misapplied or unused ability.   In his walk, Harris was a man of genius, and he let slip no opportunity to maintain his pre-eminence.   Although unwilling to detract from the fame of old Lumpy, I must here observe upon the difference in these two men with regard to pitching their wickets. Lumpy would uniformly select a point where the ball was likely to shoot, that is, over the brow of a little hill ; and when by this fore-thought and contrivance the old man would prove successful in bowling his men out, he would turn round to his party with a little grin of triumph ; nothing gratified him like this reward of his knowingness.   Lumpy, however, thought only of himself in choosing his ground ;   his fellow bowler might take his chance ;   this was neither wise nor liberal.   Harris, on the contrary, as I have already observed, considered his partner ; and, in so doing, the main chance of the game.   Unlike Lumpy, too, he would choose a rising ground to pitch the ball against, and he who is well acquainted with the game of cricket will at once perceive the advantage that must arise from a wicket pitched in this way to such a tremendous bowler as Harris was.   If I were urged to draw a comparison between these two great players, the greatest certainly in their department I ever saw, I could do it in no other way than the following :—Lumpy's ball was always pitched to the length, but delivered lower than Harris's, and never got up so high ;   he was also slower than Harris, and lost his advantage by the way in which he persisted in pitching his wicket ;   yet I think he would bowl more wickets down than the other, for the latter never pitched his wicket with this end in view ;   almost all his balls, therefore, rose over the wicket ;   conse-quently, more players would be caught out from Harris than Lumpy, and not half the number of runs got from his bowling.   I passed a very pleasant time with Harris when he came to my father's house at Hambledon, by invitation, after an illness, and for the benefit of the change of air.   Being always his companion in his walks about the neighbourhood, I had full opportunity of observing the sweetness of his disposition ;   this, with his manly contempt of every action that bore the character of meanness, gained him the admiration of every cricketer in Hambledon.

In concluding my recollections of Harris, I had well nigh omitted to say something of his skill in the other departments of the game. The fact is, the extraordinary merit of his bowling would have thrown any other fair accomplishments he might possess into the shade ; but, indeed, as a batter, I consider him rather an indifferent hand : I never recollect his getting more than 10 runs, and those very rarely. Neither was his fielding remarkable. But he was game to the back-bone, and never suffered a ball to pass him without putting his body in the way of it. If I recollect, he generally played slip.

THE FREEMANTLES. There were two of them, and, I believe, brothers. JOHN and ANDREW were their names. One was an acknowledged player long before the other began. I am now, however, speaking of Freemantle the bowler. He, with Andrew, came from some town between Winchester and Allsford. John was a stoutly-made man ; his standard about five feet ten inches. He delivered his ball high and well, and tolerably fast, yet he could not be ranked among the fast bowlers. The best compliment I can pay him is, that he was reckoned very successful, and, moreover, that his being a member of the Hambledon Club was sufficient guarantee for his general ability, as those sound and experienced judges would never admit as member any man who did not possess some qualifications above the common level.

As a batter, John Freemantle would have been reckoned a good hand in any club. He would now and then get many runs ; yet, withal, he could by no means be pronounced a *fine* batter. As a man, he bore a high character for straight-forward manly integrity ; in short, he was a hearty John Bull, and flinched no more from doing his duty than he did from a ball in the field, and this he never did, however hard it might hit him.

Andrew was a shortish, well-set man, and a left-handed player. He was an uncommonly safe, as well as good hitter ; and few wickets that I could name were more secure than Andrew's. He would often get long hands, and against the best bowling too ; and when he had once warmed into his hitting, it was a deuced hard matter to get him out—an accident would frequently do the business. In his general style of batting he very much reminded me of Aylward, who has been spoken of some pages back. He usually played the long field, and was remarkably steady and safe in this department. But Andrew Freemantle could be depended upon, whatever he might undertake, whether in cricket or in his worldly dealings.

Upon one occasion when I had come up to London, I heard of a match being played in Lord's Ground, and of course made one of the spectators of my beloved amusement. Andrew Freemantle was in, and one of the new-fashioned bowlers, commonly called throwers, was bowling to him. His name was WELLS, and I believe

he came out of Sussex. He was the first I had seen of the new
school, after the Walkers had attempted to introduce the system in
the Hambledon Club. Wells frequently pitched his balls to the
off-side of the wicket to Freemantle's left-handed hitting, who got
in before the wicket, and hit the thrower's bowling behind him.
Now, had he missed the ball, and it had hit his leg, although before
the wicket, he would not have been out, because it had been pitched
at the outside of the off-stump. I mention this trifling circumstance
to show the knowledge the latter had of the game.

Andrew Freemantle's fielding was very fair ; his post was
generally the long field. He, however, must be so well known to
many of the Mary-le-bone men now living, that I need enumerate
no more of the peculiar characteristics of his playing.

Next comes that deservedly esteemed character, JOHN SMALL,
son, and worthy successor to the celebrated batter of the same name.
He, as well as his father, was a native of Petersfield. Young Small
was a very handsomely made man. For perfect symmetry of form,
and well-knit, compact limbs and frame, his father was one of the
finest models of a man I ever beheld ; and the son was little inferior
to him in any respect. Jack Small ! my old club fellow ! when the
fresh and lusty May-tide of life sent the blood gamboling through our
veins like a Spring runlet, we have had many a good bout together :
        ' But now my head is bald, John,
            And locks as white as snow,"—
and your's have, doubtless, bleached under the cold hand of mayhap
three score winters and more ; but the churl has not yet touched
the citadel. My heart is as sound as ever, and beats regular and
true time to the tune of old and grateful thoughts for long friend-
ships. You, I am sure, can echo this sentiment. You are a musician
as well as a friend, and know the value of steadiness in both characters. I think we could give some of the young whipsters a little
trouble even now. Like the old Knight of the Boar's Head, we
might need the *legs* of these Harry Monmouths ; but it is my
opinion we could bother them yet, at a good stand to our post.
They would find some trouble to bowl down our stumps. They
say, Jack, you were born with a bat in your hand. I can believe
the tale, for I am sure you inherited the craft from both father and
mother. She, I think, took as much delight and interest in the
game as he. Many's the time I have seen that worthy woman
(every way deserving of so kind and excellent a husband) come
galloping up the ground at a grand match, where he was to play
(for, you know, she always accompanied him to those high solemn-

ities), and no player even could show more interest in the progress of the game than she, and certainly, no one, as was natural, felt so much pride in her husband's fine playing.

I do not remember, John, that you were much of a bowler, but I remember that you were everything else, and that your judgment of the game was equal to that of any man. Your style of hitting, to my mind, was of the very first quality ; and I can name no one who possessed a more accurate judgment of a short run. By the bye—is that account true which I have heard, that upon one occasion, at Mary-le-bone, you and Hammond went in first, when there were only forty runs to get to win the match ; and that you made an agreement together to run whenever the ball passed the wicket keeper : that you did this, and between you got the whole forty runs before you were out ? I have been told this anecdote of you both, and, if true, it clearly shows, according to my opinion that the judgment of the people who played against you must have been strangely at fault, or they might have prevented it ; for had but the long stop been well acquainted with the game, he would have put you out.

I always admired your fielding, Jack : I am not sure that your middle wicket (the post that your father occupied) was not as good as his—though, I dare say, you would not allow this. Certain am I that a better never was put at that post. And now, farewell, my old club-fellow.

Reader ! in a few words (now he has left the room), I assure you that in every way he was as complete a chap as I ever knew—a genuine chip of the old block—an admirable player, and a highly honourrable man. The legs at Mary-le-bone never produced the least change in him ; but, on the contrary, he was thoroughly disgusted at some of the manoeuvres that took place there from time to time.

About the time that John Small had risen into the celebrity I have just been describing, his father and Nyren retired from the field. I cannot do better, in concluding these brief recollections, than enumerate the most eminent players in the Hambledon Club when it was in its glory.

DAVID HARRIS	JOHN SMALL, Jun.	NOAH MANN
JOHN WELLS	HARRY WALKER	3 —— SCOTT
1 —— PURCHASE	TOM WALKER	4 —— TAYLOR
WILLIAM BELDHAM	2 —— ROBINSON	

No eleven in England could have had any chance with these men ; and I think they might have beaten any two-and-twenty.

[1 Richard.   2 Robert.   3 Thomas.   4 Thomas.   (Ed.)]

A FEW MEMORANDA RESPECTING THE
PROGRESS OF CRICKET

MR. WARD obligingly furnished me with a small MS., written some years since by an old cricketer, containing a few hasty recollections and rough hints to players, thrown together without regard to method or order. From the mass, I have been able to select a few portions, thinking that they might possess some interest with those of my readers who take a pride in the game.

From the authority before me, it appears, that about 150 years since, it was the custom, as at present, to pitch the wickets at the same distance asunder, viz., twenty-two yards. That the stumps (only one foot high, and two feet[1] wide) were surmounted with a bail. At that period, however, another peculiarity in the game was in practice, and which it is worth while to record. Between the stumps a hole was cut in the ground, large enough to contain the ball and the butt-end of the bat. In running a notch, the striker was required to put his bat into this hole, instead of the modern practice of touching over the popping crease. The wicket keeper, in putting out the striker when running, was obliged, when the ball was thrown in, to place it in this hole before the adversary could reach it with his bat. Many severe injuries of the hands were the consequence of this regulation ; the present mode of touching the popping crease was therefore substituted for it. At the same period the wickets were increased to twenty-two inches in height, and six inches in breadth, and instead of the old custom of placing the ball in the hole, the wicket keeper was required to put the wicket down, having the ball in his hand.

The following account of a match played in the year 1746 has been selected by the writer above-mentioned, in order to show the state of play at that time. It arose from a challenge given by Lord John Sackville on the part of the County of Kent, to play all England ; and it proved to be a well contested match, as will appear from the manner in which the players kept the field. The hitting, however, could neither have been of a high character, nor indeed safe, as may be gathered from the figure of the bat at that time ; which was similar to an old-fashioned dinner-knife—curved at the back, and sweeping in the form of a volute at the front and end. With such a bat, the system must have been all for hitting ;

[1] There must be a mistake in this account of the width of the wicket. J. N.

it would be barely possible to block ; and when the practice of bowling length balls was introduced, and which gave the bowler so great an advantage in the game, it became absolutely necessary to change the form of the bat, in order that the striker might be able to keep pace with the improvement. It was therefore made straight in the pod ; in consequence of which, a total revolution, it may be said a reformation too, ensued in the style of play.

The following is the record of the match alluded to.

KENT AGAINST ALL ENGLAND

PLAYED IN THE ARTILLERY GROUND, LONDON

England, 1st *Innings* / 2nd *Innings*

	Runs			Runs		
Harris	0	B. by	Hadswell.	4	B. by	Mills.
Dingate	3	B.	ditto	11	B.	Hadswell.
Newland	0	B.	Mills.	3	B.	ditto
Cuddy	0	B.	Hadswell.	2	C.	Danes.
Green	0	B.	Mills.	5	B.	Mills.
Waymark	7	B.	ditto	9	B.	Hadswell.
Bryan	12	S.	Kips.	7	C.	Kips.
Newlands	18	—	not out.	15	C.	Lord J. Sackville.
Harris	0	B.	Hadswell.	1	B.	Hadswell.
Smith	0	C.	Bartrum.	8	B.	Mills.
Newland	0	B.	Mills.	5	—	not out.
Byes	0			Byes 2		
	40			70		

Kent, 1st *Innings* / 2nd *Innings*

	Runs			Runs		
Lord J. Sackville	5	C. by	Waymark.	0	B. by	Harris.
Long Robin	7	B.	Newland.	9	B.	Newland.
Mills	9	B.	Harris.	6	C.	ditto
Hadswell	0	B.	ditto	5	—	not out.
Cutbush	3	C.	Green.	7	—	not out.
Bartrum	2	B.	Newland.	0	B.	Newland.
Danes	6	B.	ditto	0	C.	Smith.
Sawyer	0	C.	Waymark.	5	B.	Newland.
Kips	12	B.	Harris.	10	B.	Harris.
Mills	7	—	not out.	2	B.	Newland.
Romney	11	B.	Harris.	8	C.	Harris.
Byes	0			Byes 3		
	53			58		

Some years after this, the fashion of the bat having been changed
to a straight form, the system of stopping, or blocking, was adopted ;
when JOHN SMALL, Sen., of Petersfield, in Hampshire, became
signalized as the most eminent batsman of his day, being a very
safe player, and a remarkably fine hitter : and EDWARD STEVENS,
or, as he was commonly called, LUMPY, was esteemed the best
bowler.

About the years 1769 and 1770, the Hambledon Club, having
had a run of ill success, was on the eve of being dissolved. It had
been hitherto supported by the most respectable gentlemen in that
part of the county. They determined, however, once more to try
their fortune, and on the 23rd September, 1771, having played the
County of Surrey, at Laleham Burway, they beat them by one run.
Out of fifty-one matches played by the same club against England,
etc., during the ensuing ten years, they gained twenty-nine of
the number.

Several years since (I do not recollect the precise date) a player,
named White, of Ryegate, brought a bat to a match, which being
the width of the stumps, effectually defended his wicket from the
bowler : and in consequence, a law was passed limiting the future
width of the bat to $4\frac{1}{4}$ inches.[1] Another law also decreed that the
ball should not weigh less than $5\frac{1}{2}$ oz., or more than $5\frac{3}{4}$ oz.

On the 22nd of May, 1775, a match was played in the Artillery
Ground, between five of the Hambledon Club, and five of All
England ; when Small went in the last man for fourteen runs, and
fetched them. Lumpy was bowler upon the occasion ; and it
having been remarked that his balls had several times passed
between Small's stumps, it was considered to be a hard thing upon
the bowler that his straightest balls should be thus sacrificed ; the
number of the stumps was in consequence increased from two to
three. Many amateurs were of opinion at the time, that the alteration would tend to shorten the game : and subsequently, the
Hampshire gentlemen did me the honour of taking my opinion
upon this point. I agreed with them that it was but doing justice
to the bowler ; but I differed upon the question that it would
shorten the game ; because the striker, knowing the danger of
missing one straight ball with three instead of two stumps behind
him, would materially redouble his care ; while every loose, hard
hitter would learn to stop, and play as safe a game as possible. The

---

[1] I have a perfect recollection of this occurrence ; also, that subsequently an iron
frame, of the statute width, was constructed for, and kept by the Hambledon Club ;
through which any bat of suspected dimensions was passed, and allowed or rejected
accordingly. J. N

following record of a match, played shortly afterwards between the Hambledon Club and All England, at Sevenoaks, will prove whether my opinion was well- or ill-founded.

It was upon this occasion that Aylward fetched the extraordinary number of 167 runs from his own bat ; one of the greatest feats upon record in the annals of cricket ; for, it must be borne in mind, that his success did not arise from any loose playing or incompetence on the part of his opponents—there would then have been no merit in the triumph ; but he had to stand against the finest bowling of the day—that of Lumpy.

The reader will not fail likewise to remark the difference of amount in the score between the first and second innings on the England side : the men were either disheartened at the towering pre-eminence of the adverse party ; or, which is more probable, the latter, like good generals, would not throw away a single chance ; but although the odds were so greatly in their favour, they, instead or relaxing, or showing any indifference, fielded with still greater care than in the first innings ; and in consequence their opponents did not score half their previous number of runs. This is the genuine spirit of emulation.

HAMBLEDON CLUB AGAINST ALL ENGLAND

PLAYED 18TH JUNE, 1777

England,	1st *Innings*			2nd *Innings*		
	Runs			Runs		
Duke of Dorset	0	B.	by Brett.	5	C.	by Lord Tankerville.
Lumpy	1	B.	ditto	2	——	not out.
Wood	1	B.	ditto	1	B.	Nyren.
White	8	C.	Veck.	10	——	not out.
Miller	27	C.	Small.	23	B.	Brett.
Minchin	60	——	not out.	12	B.	Taylor.
Bowra	2	B.	Brett.	4	B.	ditto
Bullen	13	C.	Ld. Tankerville.	2	B.	Nyren.
Booker	8	C.	Brett.	2	B.	Brett.
Yalden	6	C.	Small.	8	C.	Nyren.
Pattenden	38	B.	Brett.	0	C.	Brett.
Byes	2			Byes 0		
	166			69		

Hambledon, 1st *Innings*

Runs

Lord Tankerville	3	B. by Wood.
Lear	7	B. ditto
Veck	16	B. Lumpy.
Small	33	C. White.
Francis	26	C. Wood.
Nyren	37	B. Lumpy.
Sueter	46	B. Wood.
Taylor	32	C. Bullen.
Aburrow	22	C. Minchin.
Aylward	167	B. Bullen.
Brett	9	—— not out.
Byes	5	

403

Won by Hambledon by 168 runs in *one* innings.

In the year 1778, HARRIS, the best bowler ever known, began playing in the first matches ; and from the vast superiority of his style, the hitting increased both in safety and severity, particularly in Hampshire and Surrey, where the players had an opportunity of practising against the bowling of this remarkable man.   He had a very high delivery of the balls, and was as steady to a length.   This obliged the striker to play forward, otherwise, from the rapidity of the balls rising from the ground, he was sure to be caught out at the point of the bat.   I consider cricket to have been at its zenith at the time that Harris was in prime play.

After his death, a childish mode of bowling was adopted ; very slow and high, and scarcely passing the wicket.   By some, the ball was delivered with a straight arm, nearly approaching to a gentle throw.   That practice, however, (of throwing) was set aside, by a resolution of the Mary-le-bone Club.[1]

(Here follow some general instructions to the bowler and striker ; they are, however, brief, and at the same time bear so closely upon those already given in previous pages of this little work, that the inserting of them would amount almost to a verbal repetition.

The following hints to the directors and managers of a match will amuse some readers, and not be wholly unworthy the attention of those who are ambitious of playing a keen and manœuvring, rather than a plain and straight-forward game.)

[1] Tom Walker was the first who introduced the system of throwing ; and it was to provide against such an innovation that the law was passed, and which law is still in force, although it is daily infringed, and will, in all probability, become a dead letter. J. N.

Figure 5. Title-page illustration from *Surry triumphant: or the Kentish-mens defeat*, published in 1773.

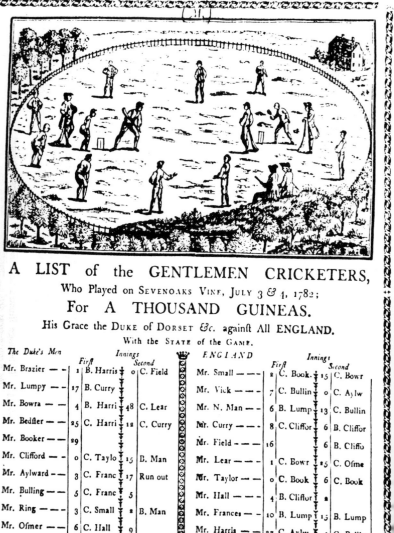

A LIST of the GENTLEMEN CRICKETERS,

Who Played on SEVENOAKS VINE, JULY 3 & 4, 1782;

For A THOUSAND GUINEAS.

His Grace the DUKE of DORSET &c. against All ENGLAND.

With the STATE of the GAME.

The Duke's Men	First	Innings	Second	
Mr. Brazier — —	1	B. Harris	0	C. Field
Mr. Lumpy — —	17	B. Curry		
Mr. Bowra — —	4	B. Harri	48	C. Lear
Mr. Bedsler — —	25	C. Harri	12	C. Curry
Mr. Booker — —	29			
Mr. Clifford — —	0	C. Taylo	15	B. Man
Mr. Aylward — —	3	C. Franc	17	Run out
Mr. Bulling — —	5	C. Franc	5	
Mr. Ring — — —	3	C. Small	2	B. Man
Mr. Ofmer — —	6	C. Hall	9	
Mr. Pattenden —	7	B. Man		
Bye Runs —	2			
. Total	102			

ENGLAND	First	Innings	Second	
Mr. Small — — —	2	C. Book.	15	C. Bowr
Mr. Vick — — —	7	C. Bullin	0	C. Aylw
Mr. N. Man — —	6	B. Lump	13	C. Bullin
Mr. Curry — — —	8	C. Cliffor	6	B. Cliffor
Mr. Field — — —	16		6	B. Cliffo
Mr. Lear — — —	1	C. Bowr	25	C. Ofme
Mr. Taylor — —	0	C. Book	6	C. Book
Mr. Hall — — —	4	B. Cliflor	2	
Mr. Frances — —	10	B. Lump	15	B. Lump
Mr. Harris — —	27	C. Aylw	1	C. Bullin
Mr. Suter — — —	5	C. Bullin	48	B. Cliffo
Bye Runs—	1		3	
.	87	140		

; Oaks Printed

Figure 6. Scorecard recording the state of the game after the second day's play of a match between Kent (His Grace the Duke of Dorset &c.) and All England in 1782.

MANAGEMENT OF A MATCH ✗

In making a match, you should be careful to stand on higher terms than you have an absolute occasion for ; that you may the more easily obtain such as are necessary ; keeping in mind the old adage—" A match well made is half won."

In pitching the wickets,[1] when it falls to your lot to have the pitching of them, you must be careful to suit your bowling. If you have one slow, and one fast bowler, pitch your wickets right up and down the wind. A slow bowler can never bowl well with the wind in his face. If your bowling is all fast, and your opponents have a slow bowler, pitch your wickets with a cross wind, that you may in some degree destroy the effect of the slow bowling. If either of your bowlers twist his balls, favour such twist as much as possible by taking care to choose the ground at that spot where the ball should pitch its proper length, a little sloping inwards.

If you go in first, let two of your most safe and steady players be put in, that you may stand a chance of " milling " the bowling in the early part of the game. And whenever a man is put out, and if the bowling have become loose, put in a resolute hard hitter. Observe also, if two players are well in, and warm with getting runs fast, and one should happen to be put out, that you supply his place immediately lest the other become cold and stiff.

When your party takes the field, let your bowlers take full time between their balls ; keeping a close field till your opponents begin to hit freely, when you must extend your men as occasion may require.

If the opposite party hold in, and are getting runs too fast, change your worst bowler, being careful at the same time to bring forward one as opposite to him as possible, both in speed and delivery. If you bring forward a fast bowler as a change, contrive, if fortune so favour you, that he shall bowl his first ball *when a cloud is passing over ;* because, as this trifling circumstance frequently affects the sight of the striker, you may thereby stand a good chance of getting him out.

When it is difficult to part two batsmen, and either of them has a favourite hit, I have often succeeded in getting him out by opening the field where his hit is placed, at the same time hinting to the bowler to give him a different style of ball. This, with the opening

[1]Now the province of the umpires ; see copy of the Laws.

of the field, has tempted him to plant his favourite hit, and in his anxiety to do so has not unfrequently committed an error fatal to him.

Every manœuvre must be tried in a desperate state of the game ; but, above all things, be slow and steady, being also especially careful that your field do not become confused. Endeavour by every means in your power, such as by changing the bowling, by little alterations in the field, or by any excuse you can invent, to delay the time, that the strikers may become cold and inactive. And when you get a turn in your favour, you may push on the game a little faster ; but even then be not too flushed with success, but let your play be still cool, cautious, and steady.

If your party go in the last innings for a certain number of runs, always keep back two or three of your safest batsmen for the last wickets. Timid or hazardous hitters seldom do so well when the game is desperate, as those who, from safe play, are more confident.

LIST OF THE MEMBERS
OF THE
MARY-LE-BONE CLUB

Acheson, Viscount
Adamson, Mr.
Aislabie, Mr. B.
Anderson, Mr.
Anderson, Mr. D.
Ashley, Hon. H.
Antrobus, Mr. J.
Baker, Mr.
Barclay, Mr. R.
Barham, Mr.
Barham, Mr. W.
Barnard, Mr.
Barnett, Mr. James
Barnett, Mr. Charles
Barnett, Mr. G. H.
Bathurst, Sir F.
Bayley, Mr. J.
Beauclerk, Lord F.
Beauclerk, Mr.
Bearblock, Mr. W.
Belfast, Earl of
Bennett, Mr.
Berens, Mr. R.
Biddulph, Mr. R. M.
Bligh, Hon. Gen.
Brooke, Mr. F. C.
Brooks, Mr.
Budd, Mr.
Balfour, Captain
Blake, Mr. J. G.
Caldwell, Mr.
Caldwell, Mr. B.
Calmady, Mr.
Campbell, Mr.
Castlereagh, Lord
Cheslyn, Mr.

Chesterfield, Earl of
Chichester, Earl of
Clitheroe, Mr. J. C.
Clonbrock, Lord
Codrington, Captain
Colomb, Major
Cope, Sir John, Bart.
Cotton, Sir St. Vin-
cent
Cox, Mr.
Cox, Mr. C.
Curtis, Sir William
Curzon, Hon. F.
Clayton, Captain
Darnley, Earl of
Davidson, Mr. H.
Davidson, Mr. D.
Davidson, Mr. W.
Davidson, Captain
Deedes, Mr. W.
Deedes, Mr. James
Delme, Mr. C.
Denne, Mr. T.
Dunlo, Lord
Dyke, Mr. P. H.
Dillon, Hon. Mr.
Ellis, Mr. W.
Ellis, Mr. C.
Everett, Mr.
Exeter, Marquis of
Fairfield, Mr. G.
Fairlie, Mr.
Fairlie, Mr. W.
Fitzroy, Mr. H.
Forbes, Mr.
Franklyn, Mr.

Fryer, Mr.
Fuller, Mr.
Finch, Hon. D.
Flayer, Mr.
Gardiner, Colonel
Gaselee, Mr.
Gibbon, Sir John, Bt.
Glenorchy, Lord
Gordon, Hon. Fred.
Gordon, Hon. Francis
Greenwood, Captain
 (2nd Life Guards)
Greenwood, Captain
 (Grenadier Guards)
Greville, Captain
Greville, Hon R. F.
Grey, Lord
Goring, Mr. F.
Grimstead, Mr.
Grimston, Lord
Grimston, Hon. E. H.
Gunning, Sir R. H.,
 Bart.
Hale, Mr. C.
Harman, Mr. E. D.
Harrington, Mr.
Heathcote, Mr. J. M.
Hemming, Mr.
Hill, Mr. C.
Hill, Mr. P.
Hillsborough, Earl of
Hoare, Mr.
Howard, Mr.
Jenner, Mr. H.
Jones, Mr. D. H.
Johnson, Mr.
Keen, Mr.
Kingscote, Mr. H.
Knatchbull, Mr.
Knight, Mr. E.
Knight, Mr. G. T.
Kynaston, Mr.

Labalmondiere, Mr.
Ladbrook, Mr. F.
Lascelles, Hon. Col.
Lascelles, Hon. E.
Leathes, Mr.
Lloyd, Mr. H.
Lloyd, Mr. C.
Loftus, Captain
Long, Colonel
Lowther, Hon. Col.
Mackinnon, Mr. H.
McTaggert, Mr. T.
Mann, Colonel
Mallet, Sir Alexander
Martyn, Mr.
Mellish, Mr. T.
Meyrick, Mr. F.
Mills, Mr. E.
Mills, Mr. C.
Montague, Hon. S. D.
Moreton, Hon. H.
Morgan, Mr. C.
Morgan, Mr. W. H.
Musgrave, Captain
Michel, Captain
Nicole, Mr.
Northy, Captain
Oglander, Mr.
Onslow, Mr. G.
Ossory, Lord
Pack, Mr.
Parry, Mr. F.
Paul, Sir D., Bart.
Paul, Mr.
Payne, Mr. G.
Pickering, Mr.
Philipps, Mr.
Plunkett, Mr.
Plymouth, Earl of
Pocklington, Mr.
Ponsonby, Hon. G.
Powell, Mr. J. H., Jr.

Purling, Mr.
Payne, Mr. A.
Pigott, Mr. W. P.
Quarme, Mr.
Reed, Mr.
Ricardo, Mr.
Robarts, Mr.
Romilly, Mr. E.
Romilly, Mr. C.
Romilly, Mr. F.
Rothschild, Mr.
Russell, Lord C.
St. Alban's, Duke of
Scott, Mr. J. W.
Scott, Hon. W.
Sewell, Colonel
Shelley, Mr.
Sivewright, Mr. E.
Sivewright, Mr. C. K.
Stanley, Hon. Capt.
  Thomas.
Stone, Mr. R.
Stonor, Mr.
Strachan, Mr.
Strathavon, Lord
Stubbs, Mr.

Smith, Mr.
Talbot, Hon. Mr.
Tanner, Mr.
Thynne, Lord W.
Townsend, Mr.
Trevanion, Mr.
Turner, Mr.
Uxbridge, Earl of
Vigne, Mr.
Vigne, Mr. G. T.
Villiers, Hon. A.
Vivian, Mr.
Vincent, Sir F.
Walker, Mr. E.
Walpole, Mr. R.
Walton, Mr.
Ward, Mr. W.
Waterpark, Lord
Webster, Colonel
Wells, Mr. J.
Willan, Mr.
Wodehouse, Mr.
Wood, Mr.
Wright, Mr. J. D.
Walker, Mr. H.
Willoughby, Sir H.

— THE END —

ON JAMES PYCROFT'S
The Cricket Field

❦

WHEN, IN 1851, THE PUBLISHING HOUSE OF LONGMAN ISSUED A BOOK
entitled *The Cricket Field* there was little anticipation of its great
Victorian success. There was no author's name on the title-page,
no more than the reference, under the heading, to two obscure books,
and the initials J. P. after the preface, to identify the writer. Although
it was to be many times re-issued up to the 1890's and again, sump-
tuously produced and eruditely footnoted, by F. S. Ashley-Cooper
in this century, little notice was taken of it on its first appearance.
Slowly, however, as the figure on the frontispiece developed from
William Clarke to W. G. Grace, it became an accepted classic of
cricket literature. Perhaps the most amazing tribute to its acceptance
was the fact that it, a book on cricket, was published in America.
This century, however, has seen its eclipse in its original form.
Mr. Ashley-Cooper produced his limited and scholarly edition for
a specific collector-market. Only the chapter on the Hambledon
Club, the finest from the literary standpoint, has survived in any
readily available form, being the one chapter reprinted in *The
Hambledon Men.*

Here, as in the case of Nyren's book, I have omitted the specifically instructional chapters although they do not in fact form a
distinct section as does *The Young Cricketer's Tutor.* These chapters, as
whole-hearted but not always objectively critical admirers of the
book have pointed out, contain many instructional points which
are still valid for cricketers. The same, however, is true of any good
book of cricket instruction, whatever its date. It is true of Nyren's
instructional passages which were based on a technique ante-
dating Pyrcroft's by fifty years. But this information can be
obtained from any good contemporary book on cricket methods
without need for adjustment. Moreover, Pycroft's style falls below
that of Nyren and Clarke. It is, not surprisingly, Nyren who raises

Pycroft to his greatest heights of literary attainment, elsewhere he is often hardly tidy and almost always " period " in style, even, at times, extravagantly so.

Cricket historians are fortunate in Pycroft. The game, to his time, had been ill-documented and never seen in a valid perspective. A man with leisure and patience was required to provide the basis of a history of the game. Pycroft had both. No professional writer dared, for the very hope of his bread and butter, to undertake the long probing and the often inconvenient travel necessary to obtain the snatches of reminiscence which were pieced together to form the basis of this work. Few statisticians possessed Pycroft's sense of historical form, few historians his knowledge of the game, few writers his enthusiasm for cricket. The study of years went to make his book. How much of his accumulation of information could not be related is indicated by the untidy chapter which he heads " Chapter of Accidents—Miscellaneous " and also by his later book, *Cricketana* (1865). Let us be critical—despite the sympathy his enthusiasm wins from our emotions—Pycroft's great value is as a historian. Every good historian of the game has worked to a considerable extent from Pycroft and the sources he indicated : often, unjustly to his memory, they have done so without acknowledgment.

It is difficult to read *The Cricket Field* without warming to the tall West Country parson whose love of the game is apparent in every line, whose sincerity is so far beyond question and who brings his carefully gathered crumbs of information in earnest offering to the service of the sport he reveres.

Only Arthur Haygarth, who is less romantic but more precise in his notes to *Cricket Scores and Biographies*, stands with Pycroft : their contribution to the history and, hence, the whole body of cricket is not always fully recognized.

Much of the information which Pycroft supplies here is familiar by virtue of its repetition, often barely paraphrased, by other cricket writers. The extent of this information shows Pycroft's due of credit : and here it is not only in the shape it had when it was gathered, but with the original freshness still upon it, as if it were still in the hands of the delighted, single-minded man who gathered it.

JOHN ARLOTT

THE CRICKET FIELD

OR

THE HISTORY AND THE SCIENCE OF CRICKET

BY

THE REV. JAMES PYCROFT

(Chapter headings are as in 1st edition thus indicating excisions.)

Preface

THE FOLLOWING PAGES ARE DEVOTED TO THE HISTORY AND THE science of our National Game. Isaac Walton has added a charm to the Rod and Line ; Col. Hawker to the Dog and the Gun ; and Nimrod and Harry Hieover to the " Hunting Field " ; but the " Cricket Field " is to this day untrodden ground. We have been long expecting to hear of some chronicler aided and abetted by the noblemen and gentlemen of the Marylebone Club, one who should combine, with all the resources of a ready writer, traditionary lore and practical experience. But time is fast thinning the ranks of the veterans. Lord Frederick Beauclerk and the once celebrated player, the Hon. Henry Tufton, afterwards Earl of Thanet, have passed away ; and probably Sparkes, of the Edinburgh Ground, and Mr. John Goldham, hereinafter mentioned, are the only surviving players who have witnessed both the formation and the jubilee of the Marylebone Club, following as it has the fortunes of the Pavilion and of the enterprising Thomas Lord, literally through " three removes " and " one fire," from White Conduit Fields to the present Lord's.

How, then, it will be asked, do we presume to save from oblivion the records of Cricket ?

As regards the antiquity of the game, our history, is the result of patient researches in old English literature. As regards its changes and chances and the players of olden time, it fortunately happens that, some fifteen years ago, we furnished ourselves with old Nyren's account of the cricketers of his time and the Hambledon Club, and took Bentley's *Book of Matches* from 1786 to 1825 to suggest questions and test the truth of answers, and passed many an interesting hour in Hampshire and Surrey by the peat fires of those villages which reared the Walkers, David Harris, Beldham, Wells, and nearly all of the All England players of fifty years since.

Bennett, Harry Hampton, Beldham, and Sparkes, who first taught us to play—all men of the last century—have at various times contributed to our earlier annals ; while Thomas Beagley, for some days our landlord, the late Mr. Ward, and especially Mr. E. H. Budd, often our antagonist in Lansdown matches, have respectively assisted in the first twenty years of the present century.

But distinct mention must we make of one most important chronicler, whose recollections were co-extensive with the whole history of the game in its matured and perfect form—WILLIAM FENNEX. And here we must thank our kind friend the Rev. John Mitford, of Benhall, for his memoranda of many a winter's evening with that fine old player, papers expecially valuable because Fennex's impressions were so distinct, and his observation so correct, that, added to his practical illustrations both with bat and ball, no other man could so truthfully enable us to compare ancient with modern times. Old Fennex, in his declining years, was hospitably appointed by Mr. Mitford to a sinecure office, created expressly in his honour, in the beautiful gardens of Benhall ; and Pilch and Box and Bailey, and all his old acquaintances, will not be surprised to hear that the old man would carefully water and roll his little cricket-ground on summer mornings, and on wet and windy days would sit in the chimney-corner, dealing over and over again by the hour, to a partner, a very dark and dingy pack of cards, and would then sally forth to teach a long remembered lesson to some hob-nailed frequenter of the village ale-house.

Some amateurs no doubt there are who could add or replace many a link in our chain of history ; and, if they will kindly come forward, we will thankfully avail ourselves of their assistance in future editions. By such collective information we may gradually build up a full and satisfactory history of our game. For the present we disdain not to offer our work to the lovers of Cricket as an outline to fill up, or as a series of pigeon-holes for general contributions.

So much for the History : but why should we venture on the Science of the game ?

Many may be excellently qualified, and have a fund of anecdote and illustration, still not one of the many will venture on a book. Hundreds play without knowing principles ; many know what they cannot explain ; and some could explain, but fear the certain labour and cost, with the most uncertain return, of authorship. For our own part, we have felt our way. The wide circulation of our *Recollections of College Days* and *Course of English Reading* promises a patient hearing on subjects within our proper sphere ; and that in this sphere lies Cricket, we may without vanity presume to assert. For in August last, at Mr. Dark's Repository at Lord's, our little treatise on the *Principles of Scientific Batting* (Slatter, Oxford, 1835) was singled out as " the book that contained as much on Cricket as all that had ever been written, and more besides." The same character we find given to it in Blaine's *Encyclopædia of Rural Sports*. That same day did we proceed to arrange with Messrs. Longman, naturally desirous to lead a second advance movement, as we led the first, and to break the spell which we had thus been assured, had for fifteen years chained down the invention of literary cricketers at the identical point where we left off ; for not a single rule or principle has yet been published in advance of our own ; though more than one author has adopted (thinking, no doubt, the parents were dead) our ideas, and language too !

" Shall we ever make new books," asks Tristram Shandy, " as apothecaries make new mixtures, by pouring only out of one vessel into another ? "

Common modesty should have suggested to such authors the example of gipsies, who, when they steal a horse, at least pay the owner the compliment of cropping the mane and tail. And, in this, no one will suspect us of making any allusion to Mr. Felix. We could no more boast a resemblance to his book than to his play ; indeed, we both play left-handed, while we write " like other folk." " Great men have the same ideas," though we wrote first ; and, if " the force of *genius* could no further go," and our sails first took the wind, who could help it ? And now we may run parallel without meeting, except—and we care not how often—in the cricket field ; for our respective designs are now wholly different. Mr. Felix attempts but a segment ; we would comprehend the whole circle. He addresses the initiated : we bend to " the meanest capacity " ; steering, however, a middle course, that the learner may not find us too deep, nor the learned too shallow. The plain and palatable is provided for the young people, though a few things more highly seasoned appeared only a proper compliment to the old.

Like solitary travellers from unknown lands, we are naturally desirous to offer some confirmation of statements, depending other-wise too much on our literary honour. We, happily, have received the following from—we believe the oldest player of the day that can be pronounced a good player still—Mr. E. H. Budd :

" I return the proof sheets of the *History of my Contemporaries*, and can truly say that they do indeed remind me of old times. I find one thing only to correct, which I hope you will be in time to alter, for your accuracy will then, to the best of my belief, be wholly without exception :—write twenty guineas, and not twenty-five, as the sum offered, by old Thomas Lord, if any one should hit out of his ground where now is Dorset Square.

"You invite me to note further particulars for your second edition[1] : the only omission I can at present detect is this—the name of Lord George Kerr, son of the Marquis of Lothian, should be added to your list of the Patrons of the Old Surrey Players ; for his lordship lived in the midst of them at Farnham, and, I have often heard Beldham say, used to provide bread and cheese and beer for as many as would come out and practise on a summer's evening : this is too *substantial* a supporter of the Noble Game to be forgotten."

We must not conclude without grateful acknowledgments to some distinguished amateurs representing the science both of the northern and the southern counties, who have kindly allowed us to compare notes on various points of play. In all of our instructions in batting, we have greatly benefited by the assistance, in the first instance, of Mr. A. Bass of Burton, and his friend Mr. Whateley, a gentleman who truly understands " Philosophy in Sport." Then the Hon. Robert Grimston judiciously suggested some modification, of our plan. We agreed with him that, for a popular work, and one " for play hours," the lighter parts should prevail over the heavier, for, with most persons, a little science goes a long way, and, if made too weighty, our " winged words " might not fly far ; seeing, as said Thucydides, " men do find it such a bore to learn anything that gives them trouble." For these reasons we drew more largely on our fund of anecdote and illustration, which had been greatly enriched by the contributions of a most valued correspondence— Mr. E. S. E. Hartopp, and Mr. C. G. Merewether. Captain Cheslyn did our cause good service in other ways. When thus the science of batting had been reduced to its fair proportions, it was happily undertaken by the Hon. Frederick Ponsonby, not only through kindness to ourselves personally, but also, we feel assured, because he takes a pleasure in protecting the interests of the rising generation. By his advice we became more distinct in our explanations, and particularly careful of venturing on such refinements of science as, though sound in theory, may possibly produce errors in practice.

" *Tantæ molis erat* CRICETANUM *condere* CAMPUM."

[1] This appeared in the first edition. J. A.

For our artist we have one word to say : not indeed for the engravings in our frontispiece—for here, undoubtedly, we have a *striking* likeness of Pilch ; and as to Clarke, our publishers hope he will prove as good a *catch* as he ever has been : but we allude to the illustrations of attitudes. In vain did our artist assure us that a fore-shortened position would defy every attempt at ease, energy, or elegance ; and that as a batsman looks better in any point of view than as seen by the bowler, no drawings from such a position could be satisfactory. Still, we were bound to insist on sacrificing, if necessary, the effect of the picture to its utility as an illustration. The figures, pp. 128 and 149 will prove how much more effective is a side view. Our principal design is to show the position of the feet and bat with regard to the wicket, and how every hit, with one exception, the Cut, is made by no other change of attitude than results from the movement of the left foot alone.

The figure of Pilch is, by permission, copied from the plate published by Mr. Mason, of Brighton, to whose repository we have much pleasure in referring our friends for some admirable engravings of the first players and amateurs of the day.

We are also happy to call attention to a volume promised by Mr. Bolland, a member of the M.C.C. and Zingari, and able withal to convey the recollections of the Cricket Field in a lively conversational style.   J. P.

Barnstaple,
   April 15th, 1851.

CHAPTER II.

THE GENERAL CHARACTER OF CRICKET

THE game of cricket, philosophically considered, is a standing panegyric on the English character : none but an orderly and sensible race of people would so amuse themselves. It calls into requisition all the cardinal virtues, some moralist would say. As with the Grecian games of old, the player must be sober and temperate. Patience, fortitude, and self-denial, the various bumps of order, obedience, and good humour, with an unruffled temper, are indispensable. For intellectual virtues we want judgment, decision, and the organ of concentrativeness—every faculty in the free use of all its limbs—and every idea in constant air and exercise. Poor, rickety, and stunted wits will never serve : the widest shoulders are of little use without a head upon them : the cricketer wants wits down to his fingers' ends. As to physical qualifications, we require not only the volatile spirits of the Irishman *Rampant*, nor the phlegmatic caution of the Scotchman *Couchant*, but we want the English combination of the two ; though, with good generalship, cricket is a game for Britons generally : the three nations would mix not better in a regiment than an eleven ; especially if the Hibernian were trained in London, and taught to enjoy something better than what has been termed his supreme felicity, " Otium cum dig-*gin-taties*." From the southern and south-eastern counties of England the game spread—not a little owing to the Propaganda of the metropolitan clubs, which played chiefly first at the Artillery Ground, then at White Conduit Fields, and lastly at Lord's, as well as latterly at the Oval, Kennington, and on all sides of London— through all the southern half of England ; and during these last twenty years the northern counties, and even Edinburgh, have sent forth distinguished players. But considering that the comple- ment of the game is twenty-two men, besides two umpires and two scorers ; and considering also that cricket, unlike every other manly contest, by flood or field, occupies commonly more than one day ; the railways, as might be expected, have tended wonderfully to the diffusion of cricket—giving rise to clubs depending on a circle of some thirty or forty miles, as also to that club in particular under the canonised saint, John Zingari, into whom are supposed to have migrated all the erratic spirits of the gipsy tribe. The Zingari are a race of ubiquitous cricketers, exclusively gentlemen-players ; for cricket affords to a race of professionals a merry and abundant, though rather a labourious livelihood, from the time that the May-fly is up to the time the first pheasant is down. Neither must we forget the All England Eleven, who, under the generalship of Mr. Clarke of Nottingham, play numbers varying from sixteen to twenty-two in almost every county in England ; and so proud are the clubs of the honour that, besides a subscription of some 70 *l.*, and part or all of the money at the field-gate, being willingly accorded for their services, much hospitality is exercised wherever they go. This tends to a healthy circulation of the life's blood of cricket, vaccinating and inoculating every wondering rustic with the principles of the national game. Our soldiers, we said, by order of the Horse Guards, are provided with cricket-grounds adjoining their barracks ; and all of her Majesty's ships have bats and balls to astonish the cockroaches at sea, and the crabs and turtles ashore. Hence it has come to pass that, wherever her Majesty's servants have " carried their victorious arms " and legs, wind and weather permitting, cricket has been played. Still the game is essentially Anglo-Saxon. Foreigners have rarely, very rarely, imitated us. The English settlers and residents everywhere play ; but of no single cricket club have we ever heard dieted either with frogs, sour crout, or macaroni. But how remarkable that cricket is not naturalised in Ireland ! the fact is very striking that it follows the course rather of ale than whiskey. Witness Kent, the land of hops, and the annual antagonists of " All England." Secondly, Farnham, which as we shall presently show, with its adjoining parishes, nurtured the finest of the old players, as well as the finest hops—*cunabula Trojæ*, the infant school of cricketers. Witness also the Burton Clubs, assisted by our excellent friend next akin to bitter ale. Witness again Alton ale, on which old Beagley throve so well, and the Scotch ale of Edinburgh, on which John Sparkes, though commencing with the last generation, has carried on his instructions, in which we ourselves once rejoiced, into the middle of the present century. The mountain mists and " mountain dew " suit better with deer-stalking than with cricket : our game disdains the Dutch courage of ardent spirits. The brain must glow with Nature's fire, and not depend upon a spirit lamp. *Mens sana in corpore sano :* feed the body, but do not cloud the mind. You, sir, with the hectic flush, the fire of your eyes burnt low in their sockets, with beak as sharp as a woodcock's from living upon suction, with pallid fact and shaky hand—our game disdains such ghostlike votaries. Rise with the lark and scent the morning air, and drink from the bubbling rill, and then, when your veins are no longer fevered with alcohol, nor puffed with tobacco smoke—when you have rectified your illicit spirits and clarified your unsettled judgment—" come again and devour up my discourse." And you, sir, with the figure of Falstaff and the nose of Bardolf—not Christianly eating that you may live, but living that you may eat—one of the *nati consumere fruges*, the devouring caterpiller and grub of human kind : our noble game has no sympathy with gluttony, still less with the habitual " diner-out," on whom outraged nature has taken vengeance, by emblazoning what was his face (*nimium ne crede colori*), encasing each limb in fat, and condemning him to be his own porter to the end of his days. " Then I am your man—and I—and I," cry a crowd of self-satisfied youths : " sound are we in wind and limb, and none have quicker hand or eye." Gently, my friends, so far well ; good hands and eyes are instruments indispensable, but only instruments. There is a wide difference between a good workman and a bag of tools, however sharp. We must have head as well as hands. You may be big enough and strong enough, but the question is whether, as Virgil says,

> " *Spiritus intus alit, totamque infusa per artus*
> *Mens agitat molem, et magno se corpore miscet.*"

And in these lines Virgil truly describes the right sort of man for a cricketer : plenty of life in him : not barely soul enough, as Robert South said, to keep his body from putrefaction ; but, however large his stature, though he weighs twenty stone, like (we will not say Mr. Mynn), but an olden wicket-keeper, named Burt, or a certain *infant* genius in the same line, of good Cambridge town—he must, like these worthies aforesaid, have *nous* in perfection, and be instinct with sense all over. Then, says Virgil, *igneus est ollis vigor* : " they must always have the steam up," otherwise the bard would have agreed with us, they are no good in an Eleven, because—

> " *Noxia corpora tardant.*
> *Terrenique hebetant artus, moribundaque membra ;* "

that, is you must suspend the laws of gravitation before they can stir— dull clods of the valley, and so many stone of carrion ; and then Virgil proceeds to describe the discipline to render those who suffer the penalties of idleness or intemperance fit to join the chosen *few* in the cricket-field :

> " *Exinde per amplum*
> *Mittimur Elysium et pauci læta arva tenemus.*"

Figure 7. Admission ticket, The Ladies Cricket Club, 1785.

Figure 8. Admission ticket, Oxfordshire Cricket Club, 1787.

Superfluous were it to make any apology for classical quotations : above all when the English is appended. At the Universities, cricket and scholarship very generally go together. When in 1836, we played victoriously on the side of Oxford against Cambridge, seven out of our eleven were classmen, and it doubtless only to avoid an invidious distinction that " Heads *v.* Heels," as was once suggested, has failed to be an annual University match ; though the *seri studiorum*—those put to school late—would not have a chance. From all this we argue that, on the authority of ancient and the experience of modern times, cricket wants mind as well as matter, and, in every sense of the word, a good understanding. How is it that Clarke's slow bowling is too successful ? ask Bayley or Caldecourt ; or say Bayley's own bowling, or that of Lillywhite, or others not much indebted to pace. " You see, sir, they bowl with their heads." Then only is the game worthy the notice of full-grown men. " A rubber of whist," says the author of the " Diary of a late Physician," in his *Law Studies*, " calls into requisition all those powers of mind that a barrister most needs " ; and nearly as much may be said of a scientific game of cricket. Mark that first-rate bowler : the batsman is hankering for his favourite cut —no—leg stump is attacked again—extra man on leg side—right— that's the spot—leg stump, and not too near him. He is screwed up, and cannot cut away ; Point has it—persevere—try again—his patience soon will fail. Ah ! look at that ball ;—the bat was more out of the perpendicular—now the bowler alters his pace—good. A dropping ball—over-reached and all but a mistake ; now a slower pace still, with extra twist—hits furiously to leg, too soon. Leg-stump is grazed, and bail off. " You see, sir," says the veteran, turning round, " a man has no room to cut from leg-stump—is more apt to hit across from leg-stump—is often caught from leg-stump ; even " leg before wicket " comes from leg-stump—gets off his ground from leg-stump—and cannot stop so readily from leg-stump—so keep on at leg-stump with an imperfect player. It wants a very long-headed player ; aye, and one of steady habits, the result of long experience in all the chances of the game, to remain steady ball after ball. An old player, who knows what is and what is not on the ball alone can resist all the temptations that leg-balls involve. Young players are going their round of experiments, and are too fond of admiration and brilliant hits : whereas it is your upright straight players that worry a bowler—twenty-two inches of wood, by four and a quarter—every inch of them before the stumps, hitting or blocking, is ra-ther disheartening ; but the moment a

man makes ready for a leg hit, the bat points to Slip instead of to
bails, and only about five inches by four of wood can cover the
wicket ; so leg-hitting is the bowler's chance : cutting also for a
similar reason. If there were no such thing as leg-hitting, we
should see a full bat every time, a man steady on his legs, and only
one thing to think of ; and what a task a bowler would have. That
was Mr. Ward's play—good for something to the last. First-rate
straight play and free leg-hitting seldom last long together : when
once exulting in the luxurious excitement of a leg-volley, the muscles
are always on the quiver to swipe round, and the bowler sees the
bat raised more and more across wicket. So, also, it is with men
who are yearning for a cut—forming for the cut like forming for
leg-hit, aye, and almost the idea of those hits coming across the
mind, set the muscles off straight play, and give the bowler a
chance. There is a deal of head-work in bowling : once make your
batsman set his mind on one hit, and give him a ball requiring the
contrary, and he is off his guard in a moment."

" Lillywhite," said a first-rate Cambridge mathematician and
cricketer who knew him well, " has a mind that would have made
him eminent in many positions in life. The game when he plays
it is very often the bowler's head and hands against the batman's
hands alone. Of course the old professional players at last have
learnt all his manœuvres : but then it is no small praise to him
that they have had to learn it ; and he has raised the standard of
batting, and remained a first-rate bowler nearly half a century.
It will easily be understood, therefore, that there is something
highly intellectual in our noble and national pastime. But the
cricketer must possess certain qualifications, not only physical and
intellectual, but moral qualifications also ; for of what avail is
the mind to design and the hand to execute, if a sulky temper
paralyses his exertions, and throws a damp upon the field ; or if
impatience dethrones judgment, and the man hits across at good
balls, because loose balls are long in coming ; or, again, if a con-
tentious and imperious disposition leaves the cricketer all " alone
in his glory," voted the pest of every eleven."

The pest of the hunting-field is the man always thinking of his
own horse and own riding, galloping against MEN and not after
DOGS. The pest of the cricket-field is the man who bores you about
his average—his wickets—his catches ; and looks blue even at the
success of his own party. If unsuccessful in batting or fielding, he
" shuts up "—" the wretch concentred all in self." No ! Give me
the man who forgets himself in the game, and, missing a ball, does

not stop to exculpate himself by dumb show, but rattles away after it—who does not blame his partner when he is run out—who plays like play, and not like earnest—who can say good-humouredly, " runs enough I hope without mine." If such a man makes a score, players remark on all sides, " Our friend deserves luck for his good humour and true spirit of the game."

Add to all this, perseverance and self-denial, and a soul above vain glory and the applause of the vulgar. Aye, perseverance in well-doing—perseverance in a straightforward, upright, and consistent course of action. See that player practising apart from the rest. What an unpretending style of play—a hundred pounds appears to depend on every ball—not a hit for these five minutes—see, he has a shilling on his stumps, and Hillyer is doing his best to knock it off. A question asked after every ball, the bowler being invited to remind him of the least inaccuracy in hitting or danger in defence. The other players are hitting all over the field making every one (but a good judge) marvel. Our friend's reward is that in the first good match, when some supposed brilliant Mr. Dashwood has been stumped from leg ball—(he cannot make his fine hits in his ground)—bowled by a shooter or caught by that sharpest of all Points, see our persevering friend—ball after ball dropping harmless from his bat, till ever and anon a single or a double are safely played away—two figures are appended to his name ; and Caldecourt, as he puts the bails on, remarks, " We've some good cricket this morning, gentlemen."

Conceit in a cricketer, as in other things, is a bar to all improvement—the vain-glorious is always thinking of the lookers-on instead of the game, and generally is condemned to live on the reputation of one skying leg-hit, or some twenty runs off three or four overs (his merriest life is a short one) for half a season.

In one word, there is no game in which amiability and an unruffled temper is so essential to success, or in which virtue is rewarded half as much as in the game of cricket. Dishonest or shuffling ways cannot prosper ; the umpires will foil every such attempt—those truly constitutional judges, bound by a code of written laws—and the public opinion of a cricket club, militates against his preferment. For cricket is a social game. Could a cricketer play a solo, or with a dummy (other than the catapult), he might play in humour or out of humour ; but an Eleven is of the nature of those commonwealths of which Cicero said, that without some regard to the cardinal virtues, they could not possibly hold together.

The game of cricket—would that all men would remember !
—is truly a game—a recreation ; so away with pettish words and
sombre looks. " If it's play, why look so serious and unhappy ? "
said a lady once in our hearing ; and added, with that fine discern-
ment in which ladies so much excel, " cricket never appears to me
so honestly a game of play as when Mr. Charles Taylor holds the
bat—every movement is so easy, the whole field is made alive, and
his style and appearance so joyous."

Cricket is not solely a game of skill—chance has sway enough
to leave the vanquished an *if* and a *but*. A long innings bespeaks
good play ; but " out the first ball " is no disgrace. A game to be
really a game, really playful, should admit of chance as well as skill.
It is the bane of chess that its character is too severe—to lose its
games is to lose your character ; and most painful of all, to be
outwitted in a fair and undeniable contest of long headedness, tact,
manœuvring, and common sense—qualities in which no man likes
to come off second best. There stand the same mechanical pieces
alike for both ; the sole difference consists in the mind of the player.
Hence the restless nights and unforgiving state of mind that has so
often followed one checkmate. Hence that " agony of rage and
disappointment from which," said Sydney Smith, " the Bishop of
—— broke my head with a chess-board fifty years ago at college."

But did we say that ladies, famed as some have been in the
hunting field, know anything of cricket too ? Not often ; though I
could have mentioned two—the wife and daughter of the late
William Ward, all three now no more, who could tell you—the
daughter especially—the forte and the failing of every player at
Lord's. I accompanied them home one evening to see some records
of the game, to their humble abode in Connaught Terrace, where
many an ornament reminded me of the former magnificence of
the Member for the City, the Bank Director, and the great Russia
merchant, when in his mansion in the then not unfashionable
Bloomsbury Square, the banqueting room of which many a Wykehamist has cause to remember ; for when famed, as they were, for
the quickest and best of fielding, the Wykehamists had won their
annual match at Lord's, and twenty years since they but rarely
lost, Mr. Ward would bear away triumphantly the winners to end
the day with him. But talking of the ladies, to say nothing of
Miss Wills, who invented over-hand bowling, their natural powers
of criticism, if honestly consulted, would, we think, tell some home
truths to a certain class of players who seem to forget that to be a
cricketer he must be still a man ; and that a manly, graceful style

of play is worth something independently of effect on the score. Take the case of the Skating Club. Will they elect a man because, in spite of arms and legs centrifugally flying, he can do some tricks of a posture-master, however wonderful ? No ! elegance in simple movements is the first thing ; without elegance nothing counts. And so should it be with cricket. I have seen men, accounted players, quite as bad as some of the cricketers in Mr. Pip's diary. " Pray, Lovell," I once heard, " have I the right guard ? " " Guard indeed ! Yes ! keep on looking as ugly and as awkward as you are now and no man in England can bowl for fright ! " *Apropos*, one of the first hints in archery is, " don't make faces when you pull your bow." Now we do seriously entreat those young ladies into whose hands this book may fall to profess, on our authority, that they are judges of the game as far as appearance goes ; and also that they will quiz, banter, tease, lecture, never-leave-alone, and otherwise plague and worry all such brothers or husbands as they shall see enacting these anatomical contortions, which too often disgrace the game of cricket.

Cricket, we said, is a game chiefly of skill, but partly of chance. Skill avails enough for interest, and not too much for friendly feeling. No game is played in better humour—never lost till won— the game's alive till the last ball. True it is that certain evil-disposed persons will sometimes leave all proper feelings behind them ; and if conceited of their own play, or bent on mortifying their adversaries, " angry passions rise," none can wonder. But for the most part there is so little to ruffle the temper, or to cause unpleasant collision, that there is no place so free from temptation—no such happy plains or lands of innocence—as our cricket-fields. We give bail for our good behaviour from the moment that we enter them. Still is a cricket-field a sphere of wholesome discipline in obedience and good order ; not to mention that manly spirit that faces danger without shrinking, and bears disappointment with good nature. Disappointment ! and say where is there more poignant disappointment, while it lasts, than after all your practice for a match, and anxious thought and resolution to avoid every chance, and score off every possible ball, to be balked and run out, caught at the slip, or stumped even off a shooter. " The course of true love (even for cricket) never did run smooth." Old Robinson, one of the finest batsmen of his day, had six unlucky innings in succession : once caught by Hammond, from a draw ; then bowled with shooters, or picked up at short slip, the poor fellow said he had lost all his play, thinking " the fault is in ourselves, and not our stars " ; and was with difficulty persuaded to play one match more, in which—whose heart does not rejoice to hear?—he made one hundred and thirty runs.

"But as to stirring excitement," writes a friend, "what can surpass a hardly-contested match when you have been manfully playing an up-hill game, and gradually the figures on the telegraph keep telling a better and a better tale, till at last the scorers stand up and proclaim a tie, and you win the game by a single and rather a nervous wicket, or by five or ten runs." If in the field with a match of this sort, and trying hard to prevent these few runs being knocked off by the last wickets, I know of no excitement so intense for the time, or which lasts so long afterwards. The recollection of these critical moments will make the heart jump for years and years to come; and it is extraordinary to see the delight with which men call up these grand moments to memory; and to be sure how they will talk and chatter, their eyes glistening and pulses getting quicker, as if they were again finishing "that rattling good match." People talk of the excitement of a good run with the Quorn or Belvoir hunt. I have now and then tumbled in for these good things; and, as far as my own feelings go, I can safely say that a fine run is not to be compared to a good match; and the excitement of the keenest sportsman is nothing either in intensity or duration to that caused by a "near thing" at cricket. The next good run takes the place of the other; whereas hard matches, like the snow-ball, gather as they go. "This is my decided opinion; and that after watching and weighing the subject for some years. I have seen men tremble and turn pale at a near match, while through the field the deepest and most awful silence reigns, unbroken but by some nervous fieldsman humming a tune or snapping his fingers to hide his agitation."

Chapter III.

THE HAMBLEDON CLUB AND THE OLD PLAYERS

WHAT have become of the old scores and the earliest records of the game of cricket ? Bentley's *Book of Matches* gives the principal games from the year 1786 ; but where are the earlier records of matches made by Dehany, Paulett, and Sir Horace Mann ? All burnt !

What the destruction of Rome and its records by the Gauls was to Niebuhr,—what the fire of London was to the antiquary in his walk from Pudding Lane to Pie Corner, such was the burning of the Pavilion at Lord's, and all the old score books—it is a mercy that the old painting of the M.C.C. was saved—to the annalist of cricket. "When we were built out by Dorset Square," says Mr. E. H. Budd, " we played for three years where the Regent's Canal has since been cut, and still called our ground " Lord's," and our dining room " the Pavilion." Here many a time have I looked over the old papers of Dehany and Sir H. Mann ; but the room was burnt, and the old scores perished in the flames. The following are curious as the two oldest scores preserved—one of the North, and the other of the South :—

NAMES OF THE PERSONS WHO PLAYED AGAINST SHEFFIELD in 1771 at Nottingham and 1772 at Sheffield.

Nottingham, Aug. 26, 1771.	Sheffield, June 1, 1772.
Huthwayte.	Coleman.
Turner.	Turner.
Loughman.	Loughman.
Coleman.	Roe.
Roe.	Spurs.
Spurr.	Stocks.
Stocks.	Collishaw.
Collishaw.	Troop.
Troop.	Mew.
Mew.	Bamford.
Rawson.	Gladwin.

Sheffield		Nottingham	
1st Inn.	81	1st Inn.	76
2nd	62	2nd	112
3rd	105		
	248		188

Nottingham		Sheffield	
1st Inn.	14	Near	70

Tuesday, 9 o'clock a.m. commenced, 8th man 0, 9th 5, 1 to come in, and only 60 a head, when the Sheffield left the field.

Nottingham gave in.

KENT AGAINST ALL ENGLAND

PLAYED IN THE ARTILLERY-GROUND, LONDON, 1746

(The score of this game is given by Nyren, see page 45.)

AND now the oldest chronicler is Nyren, who wrote an account of the cricketers of his time. The said Old Nyren borrowed the pen of our kind friend Charles Cowden Clarke, to whom John Keats dedicated an epistle, and who rejoiced in the friendship of Charles Lamb : and none but a kindred spirit to Elia could have written like " Nyren." Nyren was a fine old English yeoman, whose chivalry was cricket ; and Mr. Clarke has faithfully recorded his vivid descriptions and animated recollections. And, with his charming little volume in hand, and inkhorn at my button, in 1837 I made a tour among the cottages of William Beldham, and the few surviving worthies of the same generation ; and, having also the advantage of a MS. by the Rev. John Mitford, taken from many a winter's evening with Old Fennex, I am happy to attempt the best account that the lapse of time admits, of cricket in the olden time.

From a MS. my friend received from the late Mr. William Ward, it appears that the wickets were placed twenty-two yards apart as long since as the year 1700 ; that stumps were then only one foot high, but two feet wide. The width some persons have doubted ; but it is rendered credible by the auxiliary evidence that there was, in those days, width enough between the two stumps for cutting the wide blockhole already mentioned, and also because—whereas now we hear of stumps and bails—we read formerly of " two stumps with one stump laid across."

We are informed, also, that putting down the wickets to make a man out in running, instead of the old custom of popping the ball into the hole, was adopted on account of severe injuries to the hands, and that the wicket was changed at the same time—1779-1780—to the dimensions of twenty-two inches by six, with a third stump added.

Before this alteration the art of defence was almost unknown : balls often passed over the wicket, and often passed through. At the time of the alteration Old Nyren truly predicted that the innings would not be shortened but better played. The long pod and curved form of the bat, as seen in the old paintings, was made only for hitting, and for ground balls too. Length balls were then by no means common ; neither would low stumps encourage them : and even upright play was then practised by very few. Old Nyren relates that one Harry Hall, a ginger-bread baker of Farnham, gave peripatetic lectures to young players, and always insisted on keeping the left elbow well up ; in other words, on straight play. " Now-a-days," said Beldham, " all the world knows that ; but when I began there was very little length bowling, very little straight play, and little defence either." Fennex, said he, was the first who played out at balls ; before his day batting was too much about the crease. Beldham said that his own supposed tempting of Providence consisted in running in to hit. " You do frighten me there jumping out of your ground," said our Squire Paulett : and Fennex used also to relate how, when he played forward to the pitch of the ball, his father " had never seen the like in all his days " ; the said days extending a long way back towards the beginning of the century. While speaking of going in to hit, Beldham said, " My opinion has always been that too little is attempted in that direction. Judge your ball, and, when the least overpitched, go in and hit her away." In this opinion Mr. C. Taylor's practice would have borne Beldham out, and a fine dashing game this makes, only it is a game for none but practised players. When you are perfect in your ground, then, and then only, try what you can do out of it, as the best means to scatter the enemy and open the field.

" As to bowling," continued Beldham, " when I was a boy (say 1780), nearly all bowling was fast, and all along the ground. In those days the Hambledon Club could beat all England ; but our three parishes around Farnham beat Hambledon."

It is quite evident that Farnham was the cradle of cricketers. " Surrey," in the old scores, means nothing more than the Farnham parishes. This corner of Surrey, in every match against All England, was reckoned as part of Hampshire, and Beldham truly said " you find us regularly on the Hampshire side in Bentley's Book."

" I told you, sir," said Beldham, " that in my early days all bowling was what we called fast, or at least a moderate pace. The first lobbing slow bowler I ever saw was Tom Walker. When, in 1792, England played Kent, I did feel so ashamed of such baby bowling ; but, after all, he did more than even David Harris himself. Two years after, in 1794, at Dartford Brent, Tom Walker, with his slow bowling, headed a side against David Harris, and beat him easily."

" Kent, in early times, was not equal to our counties. Their great man was Crawte, and he was taken away from our parish of Alresford by Mr. Amherst, the gentleman who made the Kent matches. In those days, except around our parts, Farnham and the Surrey side of Hampshire, a little play went a long way. Why, no man used to be more talked of than Yalden, and when he came among us we soon made up our minds what the rest of them must be. If you want to know, sir, the time the Hambledon Club was formed, I can tell by this—when we beat them in 1780, I heard Mr. Paulett say, ' Here have I been thirty years raising our club, and are we to be beaten by a mere parish ? ' so there must have been a cricket club that played every week regularly, as long ago as 1750. We used to go as eagerly to a match as if it were two armies fighting ; we stood at nothing if we were allowed the time ; from our parish to Hambledon is twenty-seven miles, and we used to ride both ways the same day, early and late. At last I and John Wells were about building a cart, you have heard of tax carts, sir ; well the tax was put on then, and that stopped us. The members of the Hambledon Club had a caravan to take their eleven about, and used once to play always in velvet caps. Lord Winchelsea's eleven used to play in silver laced hats, and always the dress was knee-breeches and stockings. We never thought of knocks ; and I remember I played against Browne of Brighton too. Certainly you would see a bump heave under the stocking, and even the blood came through ; but I never knew a man killed, now you ask the question, and I never saw any accident of much consequence, though many an *all but*, in all my experience. Fancy the old fashion before cricket shoes, when I saw John Wells tear a finger nail off against his shoe-buckle in picking up a ball."

" Your book, sir, says much about old Nyren. This Nyren was fifty years old when I began to play ; he was our general in the Hambledon matches, but not half a player as we reckon now. He had a small farm and inn near Hambledon, and took care of the ground."

"I remember when many things first came into the game which are common now. The law for leg before wicket was not made, nor much wanted, till Ring, one of our best hitters, was shabby enough to get his leg in the way, and take advantage of the bowlers, and when Tom Taylor, another of the best hitters did the same, the bowlers found themselves beaten, and the law was passed to make leg before wicket out. The law against jerking was owing to the frightful pace Tom Walker put on, and I believe that Harry also tried something more like the modern throwing-bowling, and caused the words against throwing also. Wills was not the inventor of that kind of round bowling ; he only revived what was forgotten or new to the young folk.

"The umpires did not formerly pitch the wickets. David Harris used to think a great deal of pitching himself a good wicket, and took much pains in suiting himself every match day."

"Lord Stowell was fond of cricket. He employed me to make a ground for him at Holt Pound."

In the last century, when the waggon and the packhorse supplied the place of the penny train, there was little opportunity for these frequent meetings of men from distant counties that now puzzles us to remember who is North and who is South, who is Surrey or who is Kent. The matches then were truly county matches, and had more of the spirit of hostile tribes and rival clans. "There was no mistaking the Kent boys," said Beldham, "when they came staring in to the Green Man. A few of us had grown used to London, but Kent and Hampshire men had but to speak, or even show themselves, and you need not ask them which side they were on." So the match seemed like Sir Horace Mann and Lord Winchelsea and their respective tenantry—for when will the feudal system be quite extinct ? and there was no little pride and honour in the parishes that sent them up, and many a flagon of ale depending in the farms or the hop grounds they severally represented, as to whether they should, as the spirit-stirring saying was, "prove themselves the better men." "I remember in one match," said Beldham, "in Kent, Ring was playing against David Harris. The game was much against him. Sir Horace Mann was cutting about with his stick among the daisies, and cheering every run—you would have thought his whole fortune (and he did always bet some hundreds) was staked upon the game ; and as a new man was going in, he went across to Ring, and said, ' Ring, carry your bat through and make up all the runs, and I'll give you 10 *l.* a year for life.' Well, Ring was out for sixty runs, and only three to tie, and four to beat, and the last man made them. It was Sir Horace who took Aylward away with him out of Hampshire, but the best bat made but a poor bailiff we heard.

" Cricket was played in Sussex very early, before my day at least ; but that there was no good play I know by this, that Richard Newland, of Slinden, in Sussex, as you say, sir, taught old Richard Nyren, and that no Sussex man could be found to play him. Now, a second rate player of our parish beat Newland easily ; so you may judge what the rest of Sussex then were. But before 1780 there were some good players about Hambledon and the Surrey side of Hampshire. Crawte, the best of the Kent men, was taken away from us ; so you will not be wrong, sir, in writing down that Farnham, and thirty miles round, reared all the best players up to my day, about 1780.

" There were some who were then called ' the old players,' and here Fennex's account quite agreed with Beldham's, including Frame and old Small, who Bennett believed by tradition to have been the man who ' found out cricket,' or brought play to any degree of perfection ; also Sueter, the wicket-keeper, who in those days had very little stumping to do, and Minshull and Colshorn, all mentioned in Nyren." " These men played puddling about their crease with no freedom. I like to see players upright and, well forward, to face the ball like a man. The Duke of Dorset made a match at Dartford Brent between ' the Old Players and the New.' You laugh sir," said this tottering silver-haired old man, " but we all were new once ; well I played with the Walkers, John Wells, and the rest of our men, and beat the old ones very easily."

" Tom Walker was the most tedious fellow to bowl to, and the slowest runner between wickets I ever saw. I have seen, in running a four, Noah Mann, as fast as Tom was slow, overtake him, pat him on the back, and say, ' Good name for you is *Walker*, for you never were a runner.' It used to be said that David Harris had once bowled him 170 balls for one run ! David was a potter by trade, and in a kind of skittle alley made between hurdles, he used to practice bowling four different balls from one end, and then picking them up he would bowl them back again. His bowling cost him a great deal of practice ; but it proved well worth his while, for no man ever bowled like him, and he was always first chosen of all the men in England. *Nil sine labore,* remember young cricketers all. ' Lambert ' (not the great player of that name), said Nyren,

' had a most deceitful and teasing way of delivering the ball ; he tumbled out the Kent and Surrey men, one after another, as if picked off by a rifle corps. His perfection is accounted for by the circumstance that when he was tending his father's sheep, he would set up a hurdle or two and bowl away for hours together.'

" There was some good hitting in those days, though too little defence. Tom Taylor would cut away in fine style, almost after the manner of Mr. Budd. Old Small was among the first members of the Hambledon Club. He began to play about 1750, and Lumpy Stevens at the same time. I can give you some notion of what cricket was in those days, for Lumpy, a very bad bat, as he was well aware, once said to me, ' Beldham, what do you think cricket must have been in those days when I was thought a good batsman ? ' But fielding was very good as far back as I can remember." Now what Beldham called good fielding must have been good enough. He was himself one of the safest hands at a catch. Mr. Budd, when past forty, was still one of the quickest men I ever played with, taking always middle wicket, and often, by swift running, doing part of long field's work. Sparks, Fennex, Bennett, and young Small, and Mr. Parry, were first rate, not to mention Beagley, whose style of long stopping in the North and South Match of 1836, made Lord Frederick and Mr. Ward justly proud of so good a representative of the game in their younger days. Albeit, an old player of seventy, describing the merits of all these men, said, " put Mr. King at point, Mr. C. Ridding long-stop, and Mr. Pickering cover, and I never saw the man that could beat either of them."

" John Wells was a most dangerous man in a single wicket match, being so dead a shot at a wicket. In a celebrated match Lord Frederick warned the Honourable H. Tuffton to beware of him ; but John Wells found an opportunity of maintaining his character by shying down from the side little more than the single stump. Tom Sheridan joined some of our matches, but he was no good but to make people laugh. In our days there were no padded gloves. I have seen Tom Walker rub his bleeding fingers in the dust ! David used to say he liked to *rind* him."

" The matches against twenty-two were not uncommon in the last century. In 1788 the Hambledon Club played two-and-twenty at Cold Ash Hill. ' Drawing ' between leg and wicket is not a new invention. Old Small, of 1750, was famous for drawing, and for the greater facility he changed the crooked bat of his day for a straight bat. There was some fine cutting before Saunders' day.

Harry Walker was the first, I believe, who brought it to perfection. The next genuine cutter, for they were very scarce (I never called mine cutting, not like that of Saunders at least), was Robinson. Walker and Robinson would wait for the ball all but past the wicket, and cut with great force. Others made good off hits, but did not hit late enough for a good cut. I would never cut with slow bowling. I believe that Walker, Fennex, and myself, first opened the old players' eyes to what could be done with the bat ; Walker by cutting, and Fennex and I by forward play : but all improvement was owing to David Harris's bowling. His bowling rose almost perpendicular : it was once pronounced a jerk ; it was altogether most extraordinary. For thirteen years I averaged forty-three a match, though frequently I had only one innings ; but I never could half play unless runs were really wanted."

CHAPTER IV.

CRICKET GENERALLY ESTABLISHED AS A NATIONAL GAME BY THE END OF THE LAST CENTURY

LITTLE is recorded of the Hambledon Club after the year 1786. It broke up when Old Nyren left it, in 1791. Though in this last year the true old Hambledon Eleven all but beat twenty-two of Middlesex at Lord's. Their cricket-ground on Broadhalfpenny Down, in Hampshire, was so far removed from the many noblemen and gentlemen who had seen and admired the severe bowling of David Harris, the brilliant hitting of Beldham, and the interminable defence of the Walkers, that these worthies soon found a more genial sphere for their energies on the grounds of Kent, Surrey, and Middlesex. Still, though the land was deserted, the men survived, and imparted a knowledge of their craft to gentles and simples far and wide.

Most gladly would we chronicle that these good men and true were actuated by a great and a patriotic spirit, to diffuse an aid to civilisation—for such our game claims to be—among their wonder-stricken fellow-countrymen ; but, in truth, we confess that " reaping golden opinions " and coins, " from all kinds of men," as well as that indescribable tumult and joyous emotions which attend the ball vigorously propelled or heroically stopped, while hundreds of voices shout applause, that such stirring motives, more powerful far with vain-glorious men than any foreshortened view of abstract virtue, tended to the migration of the pride of Hambledon. Still, doubtful though the motive, certain is the fact, that the Hambledon players did carry their bats and stumps out of Hampshire into the adjoining counties, and gradually, like all great commanders, taught their adversaries to conquer too. In some instances, as with Lord Winchelsea, Mr. Amherst, and others, noblemen combined the *utile dulci*, pleasure and business, and retained a great player as a keeper or a bailiff, as Martingell once was engaged by Earl Ducie. In other instances, the play of the summer led to employment through the winter ; or else these busy bees lived on the sweets of their sunshine toil, enjoying *otium cum dignitate*—that is, living like gentlemen, with nothing to do.

This accounts for our finding these Hampshire men playing Kent matches ; being, like a learned Lord in Punch's picture, " naturalised everywhere," or citizens of the world.

Let us trace these Hambledonians in all their contests, from the date mentioned (1786 to 1800), the eventful period of the French Revolution and Nelson's victories, and see how the Bank stopping payment, the mutiny of the fleet, and the threatened invasion, put together, did not prevent balls from flying over the tented field, in a far more innocent and rational way on this than on the other side of the water.

Now, what were the matches in the last century—" eleven gentlemen against the twelve Cæsars?" No! these, though ancient names, are of modern times. Kent and England was as good an annual match in the last as in the present century. The White Conduit Fields and the Artillery Ground supplied the place of Lord's, though in 1787 the name of Lord's is found in Bentley's matches, implying, of course, the old Marylebone Ground, now Dorset Square, under Thomas Lord, and not the present by St. John's Wood, more properly deserving the name of Dark's than Lord's. The Kentish battlefields were Sevenoaks, the land of Clout, one of the original makers of cricket-balls ; Coxheath, Dandelion Fields, in the Isle of Thanet, and Cobham Park ; also Dartford Brent and Pennenden Heath : there is also early mention of Gravesend, Rochester, and Woolwich.

Next in importance to the Kent matches were those of Hampshire and of Surrey, with each of which counties indifferently the Hambledon men used to play. For it must not be supposed that the whole county of Surrey put forth a crop of stumps and wickets all at once : we have already said that malt and hops and cricket have ever gone together. Two parishes in Surrey, adjoining Hants, won the original laurels for their county ; and those in the immediate vicinity of the Farnham hop country. The Holt, near Farnham, and Moulsey Hurst, were the Surrey grounds. The match might truly have been called " Farnham's hop-gatherers v. those of Kent." The former, aided occasionally by men who drank the ale of Alton, just as Burton-on-Trent, life-sustainer to our Indian empire, sends forth its giants, refreshed with bitter ale, to defend the honour of the neighbouring towns and counties. The men of Hampshire, after Broadhalfpenny was abandoned to docks and thistles, pitched their tents generally either upon Windmill Downs or upon Stoke Downs ; and once they played a match against T. Asheton Smith, whose mantle has descended on a worthy representative, whether on the level turf or by the cover's side. Albeit, when the gentleman has a " meet," as occasionally advertised at Hambledon, he must unconsciously avoid the spot where " titch and turn "—the Hamp-

Figure 9. Cricket played by the Gentlemen's Club at White Conduit Fields, London, now the site of Dorset Square, in 1784.

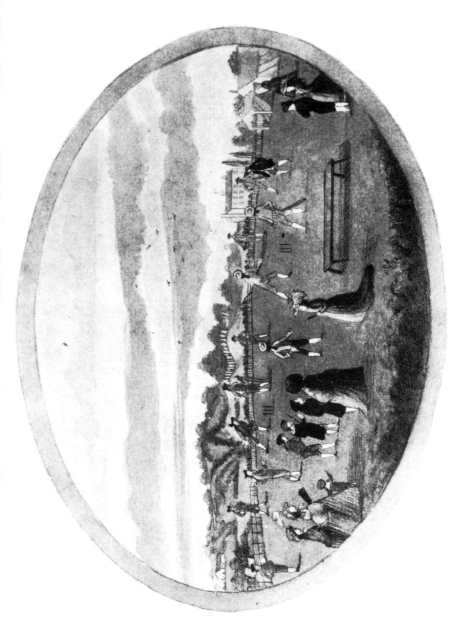

Figure 12. A game in progress at Thomas Lord's 'new

shire cry—did once exhilarate the famous James Aylward, among others, as he astonished the Farnham waggoner, by continuing one and the same innings as the man drove up on the Tuesday afternoon and down on the Wednesday morning. This match was played at Andover, and the surnames of most of the Eleven may be read on the tombstones, with the best of characters, in Andover Churchyard. Bourne Paddock, Earl Darnley's estate, and Burley Park, in Rutland-shire, constituted often the debatable ground in their respective counties. Earl Darnley, as well as Sir Horace Mann and Earl Winchelsea, Mr. Paulett and Mr. East, lent their names and patronage to Elevens ; sometimes in the places mentioned, some-times at Lord's, and sometimes at Perriam Downs, near Luggershal, in Wiltshire.

Middlesex also, exclusively of the Marylebone Club, had its Eleven in these days ; or, we should say, its *twenty-two*, for that was the number then required to stand the disciplined forces of Hampshire, Kent or England. And this reminds us of an " Uxbridge ground," where Middlesex played and lost, and " Hornchurch, Essex," where Essex, in 1791, was sufficiently advanced to win against Marylebone, an occasion memorable, because Lord Frederic Beauclerk there played his first recorded match, making scarce any runs, but bowling four wickets. " There was also," writes the Hon. R. Grimstone, " ' the Bowling-green ' at Harrow-on-the-Hill, where the school played : Richardson, who subsequently became Mr. Justice Richardson, was the captain of the School Eleven in 1782."

Already, in 1790, the game was spreading northwards, or, rather, proofs exist that it had long before struck far and wide its roots and branches in Northern latitudes ; and also that it was a game as popular with the men of labour as the men of leisure, and therefore incontestably of home growth : no mere exotic, or importation, of the favoured few can cricket be, if, like its namesake, it is found " a household word " with those whom Burns aptly calls " the many-aproned sons of mechanical life."

In 1791 Eton, that is the old Etonians, played Marylebone, four players given on either side ; and all true Etonians will thank us for informing them, not only that the seven Etonians were more than a match for their adversaries, but also that this match proves that Eton had, at that early date, the honour of sending forth the most distinguished amateurs of the day ; for Lord Winchelsea, Hon. H. Fitzroy, Earl Darnley, Hon. E. Bligh, C. Anguish, Asheton Smith —good men and true—were Etonians all. This match was played

in Burley Park, Rutlandshire, on the following day, June 25th, 1791 :
the Marylebone played eleven yeomen and artizans of Leicester ;
and though the Leicestrians cut a sorry figure, still the fact that the
Midland Counties practised cricket sixty years ago is worth recording.
Peter Heward, of Leicester, a famous wicket-keeper, of twenty years
since, told me of a trial match in which he saw his father, quite an
old man, with another veteran of his own standing, quickly put out
with the old-fashioned slow bowling for some twenty runs a really
good Eleven—good, that is, against the modern style of bowling ;
and cricket was not a new game in this old man's early days (say
1780) about Leicester and Nottingham, as the score in page 72
alone would prove ; for such a game as cricket, evidently of gradual
development, must have been played in some primitive form many
a long year before the date of 1775, in which it had excited sufficient
interest, and was itself sufficiently matured in form to show the two
Elevens of Sheffield and of Nottingham. Add to this what we have
already mentioned, a rude form of cricket as far north as Angus
and Lothian in 1700, and we can hardly doubt that cricket was
known as early in the Midland as in the Southern Counties.
The men of Nottingham—land of Clarke, Barker, and of Redgate
—next month, in the same year (1791) threw down the gauntlet,
and shared the same fate ; and next day the Marylebone, " adding,"
in a cricketing sense, " insult unto injury," played twenty-two of
them, and won by thirteen runs.

In 1790, the shopocracy of Brighton had also an Eleven ; and
Sussex and Surrey, in 1792, sent an eleven against England to
Lord's who scored the longest number in one innings on record—
453 runs ! " M.C.C. v. twenty-two of Nottingham," we now find
an annual match ; and also " M.C.C. v. Brighton," which becomes
at once worthy of the fame that Sussex long has borne. In 1793,
the old Westminster men all but beat the old Etonians ; and Essex
and Herts, too near not to emulate the fame of Kent and Surrey,
were content, like second-rate performers, to have, though playing
twenty-two, one benefit between them, in the shape of defeat in
one innings from England. And here we are reminded by two old
players, a Kent and an Essex man, that, being schoolboys in 1785,
they can respectively testify that, both in Kent and in Essex, cricket
appeared to them more of a village game than they have ever seen
it of late years. " There was a cricket-bat behind the door, or else
up in the bacon rack, in every cottage. We heard little of clubs,
except around London ; still the game was played by many or by
few, in every school and village green in Essex and in Kent, and the

field placed much as when with the Sidmouth I played the Teign-bridge Club in 1826. Mr. Whitehead was the great hitter of Kent ; and Frame and Small were names as often mentioned as Pilch and Parr by our boys now." And now (1793) the game had penetrated further West ; for eleven yeomen at Oldfield Bray, in Berkshire, had learned long enough to defeat a good eleven of the Marylebone Club.

In 1795, the Hon. Colonel Lennox, memorable for a duel with the Duke of York, fought on the cricket ground at Dartford Brent, headed Elevens against the Earl of Winchelsea ; and now, first the Marylebone eleven beat sixteen Oxonians on Bullingdon Green.

In 1797, the Montpelier Club and ground attract our notice. The name of this club is one of the most ancient, and their ground a short distance only from the ground of Hall of Camberwell.

Swaffham, in Norfolk, is now mentioned for the first time. But Norfolk, lies out of the usual road, and is a county that, as Mr. Dickens said of Golden Square, before it was the residence of Cardinal Wiseman " is nobody's way to or from any place." So, in those slow coach and pack-horse days, the patrons of Kent, Surrey, Hants, and Marylebone, who alone gave to what else were " airy nothing, a local habitation and a name," could not so easily extend their circuit to the land of turkeys, lithotomy, and dumplings. But it happened once that Lord Frederic Beauclerk was heard to say, his eleven should beat any three elevens in the county of Norfolk ; whence arose a challenge from the Norfolk men, whom, sure enough, his Lordship did beat, and that in one innings ; and a print, though not on pocket-handkerchiefs, was struck off to perpetuate this honourable achievement.

Lord F. Beauclerk was now one of the first batsmen of his day ; as also were the Hon. H. and I. Tuffton ; and frequently headed a division of the Marylebone, or some county club, against Middle-sex, and even Hampstead and Highgate.

In this year (1798) these gentlemen aforesaid made the firs attempt at a Gentlemen and Players' match ; and on this first occasion the players won ; but when we mention that they had three players given, and also that T. Walker, Beldham, and Hammond were the three, certainly it was like playing England, " the part of England being left out by particular desire."

Kent attacked England in 1798, but, being beaten in about half an innings, we find the Kentish men in 1800, though still hankering after that cosmopolitan distinction, modestly accept the odds of nineteen, and afterwards playing twenty-three men to twelve.

The chief patronage, and consequently the chief practice, in cricket, was beyond all comparison in London. There the play was nearly all professional : even the gentlemen made a profession of it ; and therefore, though cricket was far more extensively spread throughout the villages of Kent than of Middlesex, the clubs of the metropolis figure in the score books as defying all competition. Professional players, we may observe, have always a decided advantage in respect of judicious choice and mustering their best men. The best eleven Players are almost always and can be mustered on a given day. Neither favour, friendship, nor etiquette interferes with their election ; but the eleven gentlemen of England can never be anything more than the best eleven known to the party who make the match, and such as can spare the time and money which the match demands.

Having now traced the rise and progress of the game to the time of its general establishment till the time that Beldham had shown the full powers of the bat, and Lord Frederic had, as Fennex always declared, formed his style upon Beldham's ; and since now we approach the era of a new school, and the forward play of Fennex —which his father termed an innovation and presumption " contrary to all experience "—till the same forward play was proved effectual by Lambert ; and Hammond had shown that, in spite of wicket keepers, bowling, if slow especially, might be met and hit away at the pitch ; now we will wait to characterise, in the words of eye-witnesses, the heroes of the contests already mentioned.

Of the old players, I may be brief, because the few old gentlemen (with one of whom I am in daily communication) who have heard even the names of the Walkers, Frame, Small, and David Harris, are passing away, full of years, and almost all their written history consists in undiscriminating scores.

In point of style the old players did not play the steady game with maiden overs as at present. The defensive was comparatively unknown : both the bat and the wicket, and the style of bowling too, were all adapted to a short life and a merry one. The wooden substitute for a ball, as in Cat and Dog, before described, evidently implied a hitting, and not a stopping game.

The wicket, as we collect from a MS. furnished by an old friend to the late William Ward, Esq., was, in the early days of the Hambledon Club, one foot high and two feet wide, consisting of two stumps only, with one stump laid across. Thus straight balls passed between, and what we now call well pitched balls would of course rise over. Where, then, was the encouragement to block,

when fortune would so often serve the place of science ? And, as
to the bat, look at the picture of cricket as played in the old Artillery
Ground ; the bat curved at the end like a hockey stick, or the
handle of a spoon—and as common implements usually are adapted
to the work to be performed, you will readily believe that in olden
times the freest hitter was the best batsman. The bowling was
all along the ground, hand and eye being everything, and judgment
nothing, because the art originally was to bowl under the bat ; the
wicket was too low for rising balls ; and the reason we hear sometimes of the block hole was, not that the blockhole originally
denoted guard, but because between these two-feet-asunder stumps
there was cut a hole big enough to contain the ball, and, as now
with the school boy's game of rounders, the hitter was made out
in running a notch by the ball being popped into this hole (whence
popping crease) before the point of the bat could reach it.

Did we say running a notch ? *unde* notch ? What wonder ere
the days of useful knowledge, and Sir William Curtis's three R's,
or reading, writing, and arithmetic, that natural science should
be evolved in a truly natural way ; what wonder that notches on
a stick, like the notches in the milk-woman's tally in Hogarth's
picture, should supply the place of those complicated papers of
vertical columns, which subject the bowling, the batting, and the
fielding to a process severely and scrupulously just, of analytical
observation, or differential calculus. Where now there sit on
kitchen chairs, with ink bottle tied to a stump the worse for wear,
Messrs. Caldecourt and Bailey ('tis pity two such men should ever
not be umpires), with an uncomfortable length of paper on their
knees, and large tin telegraphic letters above their heads ; and
where now is Lillywhite's print press to hand down every hit as
soon as made on twopenny cards to the next generation ; there,
or in a similar position, old Frame, or young Small (young once :
he died in 1834, aged eighty) might have placed a trusty yeoman
to cut notches with his bread and bacon knife on an ashen stick.
Oh ! 'tis enough to make the Hambledon heroes sit upright in
their graves with astonishment to think that in the Gentlemen and
Players' Match, in 1850, the cricketers of old Sparks' Ground, at
Edinburgh, could actually know the score of the first innings in
London, almost as soon as the second had commenced.

But when we say that the old players had little or nothing of the
defensive, we speak of the play before 1780, when David Harris
flourished ; for William Beldham distinctly assured us that the art
of bowling over the bat by " length balls " originated with the

famous David. An assertion, we will venture to say, which requires a little, and only a little, qualification. Length bowling, or three quarter balls, to use a popular, though exploded, expression, was introduced in David's time, and by him first brought to perfection. And what rather confirms this statement is, that the early bowlers were very swift bowlers—such was not only David, but the famous Brett, of earlier date, and Frame of great renown : a more moderate pace resulted from the new discovery of a well pitched bail ball.

The old players well understood the art of twisting, or bias bowling. Lambert, " the little farmer," says Nyren, " improved on the art, and puzzled the Kent men in a great match, by twisting the reverse of the usual way—that is, from the off to leg stump." Tom Walker tried what Nyren calls the throwing-bowling, and defied all the players of the day to withstand this novelty ; but, by a council of the Hambledon Club, this was forbidden, and Wills, a Sussex man, had the praise for inventing it some twenty years later. In a notable match of the Hambledon Club, it was observed, at a critical point of the game, that the ball passed three times between the two stumps without knocking off the bail ; and then, first about 1780, a third stump was added, and, seeing that the new style of balls which rise over the bat rose also over the wickets, then but one foot high, the wicket was altered to the dimensions of 22 inches by 6, at which measure it remained till about 1814, when it was increased to 26 inches by 8, and again to its present dimensions of 27 inches by 8 in 1817.

David Harris's, bowling, Fennex used to say, introduced, or at least established and fixed, a steady and defensive style of batting. " I have seen," said Sparkes, " seventy or eighty runs in an innings, though not more than eight or nine made at Harris's end." " Harris," said an excellent judge, who well remembers him, " attained nearly all the quickness of rise and height of delivery, of the over-hand bowling, with far greater straightness and precision. The ball appeared to be forced out from under his arm with some unaccountable jerk, so that it was delivered breast high. His precision exceeded anything I have ever seen, in so much that Tom Walker declared that, on one occasion, where turf was thin, and the colour of the soil readily appeared, one spot was positively uncovered by the repeated pitching of David's balls in the same place." " This bowling," said Sparkes, " compelled you to make the best of your reach forward ; for if you let the ball pitch too near and crowd upon you, no player could possibly prevent a mistake from the height and rapidity with which it cut up from the ground."

This account agrees with the well-known description of Nyren. " Harris's mode of delivering the ball was very singular. He would bring it from under the arm by a twist, and nearly as high as his arm-pit, and with this action push it, as it were, from him. How it was that the balls acquired the velocity they did by this mode of delivery, I never could comprehend. His balls were very little beholden to the ground ; it was but a touch and up again ; and woe be to the man who did not get in to block them, for they had such a peculiar curl they would grind his fingers against the bat."

And Nyren agrees with my informants in ascribing great improvement in batting, and he specifies, " particularly in stopping " (for the act of defence, we said, was not essential to the batsman in the ideas of one of the old players), to the bowling of David Harris, and bears testimony to an assertion, that forward play, that is meeting at the pitch balls considerably short of a half volley, was little known to the oldest players, and was called into requisition chiefly by the bowling of David Harris. Obviously, with the primitive fashion of ground bowling, called sneakers, forward play could have no place, and even well-pitched balls, like those of Noah Mann, alias Lumpy, of moderate pace might be played with some effect, even behind the crease ; but David Harris, with pace, pitch, and rapid rise combined, imperatively demanded a new invention, and such was forward play about 1800. Old Fennex, who died, alas ! in a Middlesex workhouse, aged eighty, in 1839 (had his conduct been as straightforward and upright as his bat, he would have known a better end), always declared that he was the first, and remained long without followers ; and no small praise is due to the boldness and originality that set at nought the received maxims of his forefathers before he was born or thought of ; daring to try things that, had they been ordinarily reasonable, would not, of course, have been ignored by Frame, by Pinchase, nor by Small. The world wants such men as Fennex ; men, who, like the late lamented Sir Robert Peel, will shake off the prejudices of birth, parentage, and education, and boldly declare that age has taught them wisdom, and that the policy of their predecessors, however expensively stereotyped, must be revised and corrected and adapted to the demands of a more inquiring generation. " My father," said Fennex, " asked me how I came by that new play, reaching out as no one ever saw before." The same style he lived to see practised, not elegantly, but with wonderful power and effect by Lambert, " a most severe and resolute hitter " ; and Fennex also boasted that he had a most proficient disciple in Fuller Pilch : though I suspect—that as " *poeta nascitur non fit* " ; that is, that all great performers appear to have brought the secret of their excellence into the world along with them, and are not the mere puppets of which others pull the strings—that Fuller Pilch may think he rather coincided with than learnt from William Fennex.

Now the David Harris aforesaid, who wrought quite a revolution in the game, changed cricket from a backward and a slashing to a forward and defensive game, and claiming higher stumps to do justice to his skill—this David, whose bowling was many years before his generation, having all the excellence of Lillywhite's high delivery, though free from all imputation of unfairness—this David rose early, and late took rest, and ate the bread of carefulness, before he attained such distinction as, in these days of railroads, Thames tunnels, and tubular gloves and bridges, to deserve the notice of our pen. " For," said John Bennett, " you might have seen David practising at dinner time and after hours, all the winter through " ; and " many a Hampshire barn," said Beagley, " has been heard to resound with bats and balls as well as threshing." And now we must mention the men, who, at the end of the last century, represented the Pilch, the Parr, the Wenman, and the Wisden of the present day.

Lord Beauclerk was formed on the style of Beldham, whom, in brilliancy of hitting, he nearly resembled. The Hon. H. Bligh and Hon. H. Tufton were of the same school. Sir Peter Burrell was also a good hitter, and these were the most distinguished gentlemen players of the day. Earl Winchelsea was in every principal match, but rather for his patronage than his play : and the Hon. Col. Lennox for the same reason. Mr. R. Whitehead was a Kent player of great celebrity. But Lord Beauclerk was the only gentleman who had any claim in the last century to play in an All England eleven. He was also one of the fastest runners. Hammond was the great wicket-keeper ; but then the bowling was slow : Spares said he saw him catch out Robinson by a draw between leg and wicket. Freemantle was the first long stop ; but Ray the finest field in England ; and in those days, when the scores were long, fielding was of even more consideration than at present. Of the professional players, Beldham, Hammond, Tom and Harry Walker Freemantle, Robinson, Fennex, J. Wells, and J. Small were the first chosen after Harris had passed away ; for Nyren says that even Lord Beauclerk could hardly have seen David Harris in his prime At this time there was a sufficient number of players to maintair the credit of the left hands. On the 10th of May, 1790, the Left-handed beat the Right by thirty-nine runs. This match reveals that Harris and Aylward, and the three best Kent players, Brazier, Crawte, and Clifford—Sueter, the first distinguished wicket-keeper, —H. Walker, and Freemantle were all left-handed : so also was Noah Mann.

The above-mentioned players are quite sufficient to give some idea of the play of the last century. Sparkes is well known to the author of these pages as his quondam instructor. In batting he differed not widely from the usual style of good players, save that he never played forward to any very great extent. Playing under leg, according to the old fashion (we call it old-fashioned though Pilch adopts it), served instead of the far more elegant and efficient " draw." Sparkes was also a fair bias bowler, but of no great pace, and not very difficult. I remember his saying that the old school of slow bowling was beaten by Hammond setting the example of running in. " Hammond," he said, " on one occasion hit back a slow ball to Lord F. Beauclerk with such frightful force that it just skimmed his Lordship's unguarded head, and he had scarcely nerve to bowl after. Of Fennex we can also speak from our friend Rev. John Mitford. Fennex was a fair straight-forward hitter, and once as good a single wicket player as any in England. His attitude was easy, and he played elegantly, and hit well from the wrist. If his bowling was any specimen of that of his contemporaries, they were by no means to be despised. His bowling was very swift and of high delivery, the ball cut and ground up with great quickness and precision. Fennex used to say that the men of the present day had little idea of what the old underhand bowling really could effect ; and, from the specimen which Fennex himself gave at sixty-five years of age, there appeared to be much reason in his assertion. Of all the players Fennex had ever seen (for some partiality for bygone days we must of course allow) none elicited his notes of admiration like Beldham. We cannot compare a man who played underhand with those who are formed on overhand bowling. Still there is reason to believe what Mr. Ward and others have told us, that Beldham had that genius for cricket, that wonderful eye (although it failed him very early), and quickness of hand, that would have made him a great player in any age.

Beldham related to us in 1838, and that with no little nimbleness of hand and vivacity of eye, while he suited the action to the word with a bat of his own manufacture, how he had drawn forth the plaudits of Lords' as he hit round and helped on the bowling of

Browne of Brighton, even faster than before, though the good men
of Brighton thought that no one could stand against him, and
Browne had thought to bowl Beldham off his legs. This match of
Hants against England in 1819 Fennex was fond of describing, and
certainly it gives some idea of what Beldham could do. " Osbaldeston,"· said Mr. Ward, " with his tremendously fast bowling, was
defying everyone at single wicket, and he and Lambert challenged
Mr. E. H. Budd with three others. Just then I had seen Browne's
swift bowling, and a hint from me settled the match. Browne was
engaged, and Osbaldeston was beaten with his own weapons."
A match was now made to give Browne a fair trial, and " we were
having a social glass," said Fennex, " and talking over with Beldham
the match of the morrow at the " Green Man," when Browne came
in, and told Beldham, with as much sincerity as good-humour,
that he should soon send his stumps a-flying."   " Hold there,"
said Beldham, fingering his bat, " you will be good enough to allow
me this bit of wood, won't you ? "   " Certainly," said Browne.
" Quite satisfied," answered Beldham, " so to-morrow you shall
see."   " Seventy-two runs," said Fennex, and the score book
attests his accuracy, " was Beldham's first and only innings," and
Beagley also joined with Fennex, and assured us, that he never saw
a more complete triumph of a batsman over a bowler. Nearly
every ball was cut or slipped away till Browne hardly dared to
bowl within his reach.

We desire not to qualify the praises of Beldham, but when we
hear that he was unrivalled in elegant and brilliant hitting, and
in that wonderful versatility that cut indifferently, quick as lightning,
all round him, we cannot help remarking, that such bowling as
that of Redgate or Wisden renders imperatively necessary a severe
style of defence, and an attitude of cautious watchfulness, that must
render the batsman not quite such a picture for the artist as might
be seen in the days of Beldham and Lord F. Beauclerk.

So far we have traced the diffusion of the game and the degrees
of proficiency attained to the beginning of the present century. To
sum up the evidence, by the year 1800, cricket had become the
pastime even of the common people in Hampshire, Surrey, Sussex,
and Kent ; and had been introduced into the adjoining counties,
and though we cannot trace its continuity beyond Rutlandshire
and Burley Park, certainly it had been long familiar to the men of
Leicester and of Nottingham and Sheffield. That, in point of skill,
Fielding, generally, was already as good and quite as much valued
in a match as it has been since ; and Wicket-keeping in particular

had been ably executed by Sueter, for he could stump off Brett, whose pace Nyren, acquainted as he was with all the bowlers to the days of Lillywhite, called quite of the steam-engine power, albeit no wicket-keeper could shine like Wenman or Box, except with the regularity of overhand bowling ; and already Bowlers had attained by bias and quick delivery all the excellence which underhand bowling admits. Still, as regards Batting, the very fact that the stumps remained six inches wide, by twenty-two inches in height, undeniably proves that the secret of success was limited to comparatively a small number of players.

Chapter V.

THE FIRST TWENTY YEARS OF THE PRESENT CENTURY

Before this century was one year old, David Harris, Harry Walker, Purchase, Aylward, and Lumpy had left the stage, and John Small, instead of hitting bad balls whose stitches would not last a match, had learnt to make commodities so good that Clout's and Duke's were mere toy-shop in comparison. Noah Mann was the Caldecourt, or umpire, of the day, and Harry Bentley also, when he did not play. Five years more saw nearly the last of Earl Winchelsea, Sir Horace Mann, Earl Darnley, and Lord Yarmouth ; still Surrey had a generous friend in Mr. Laurell, Hants in Mr. T. Smith, and Kent in the Honourables H. and J. Tuffton. The Pavilion at Lord's, then and since 1787 on the site of Dorset Square, was attended by Lord Frederick Beauclerk, then a young man of four-and-twenty, the Honourables Colonel Bligh, General Lennox, H. and J. Tuffton, and A. Upton. Also, there were usually Messrs. R. Whitehead, G. Leycester, S. Vigne, and F. Ladbroke. These were the great promoters of the matches, and the first of the amateurs. Cricket, we have shown, was originally classed among the games of the lower orders ; so we find the yeomen infinitely superior to the gentlemen even before cricket had become by any means so much of a profession as it is now. Tom Walker, Beldham, John Wells, Fennex, Hammond, Robinson, Lambert, Sparkes, H. Bentley, Bennett, Freemantle, were the best professionals of the day. For it was seven or eight years later that E. H. Budd, and his unequal rival Mr. Brand, and his sporting friend Osbaldeston, as also that fine player, E. Parry, Esq., severally appeared ; and later still, that Mr. Ward, Howard, Beagley, Thumwood, Caldecourt, Slater, Flavel, Ashby, Searle, and Saunders, successively showed every resource of bias bowling to shorten the scores, and of fine hitting to lengthen them. By the end of these twenty years, all these distinguished players had taught a game in which the batting beat the bowling. Matches took up three days ; the wicket had been twice enlarged, once about 1814, and again about 1817 ; old Lord had tried his third, and present, ground ; the Legs had taught the wisdom of playing rather for love than money ; slow coaches had given way to fast, long whist to short, and ultimately Lambert, John Wells, Howard, and Powell, handed over the ball to Broadbridge and Lillywhite. Such is the scene, the characters, and the performance. Matches in those days were more numerously attended than now, said Mr. Ward : he thought that the old game was more attractive, because more busy, than the new. Tom Lord's flag was the well-known telegraph that brought him in from three to four thousand sixpences at a match. John Goldham, the octogenarian inspector of Billingsgate, has seen the Duke of York and his adversary, Honourable Colonel Lennox, in the same game, and had the honour of playing with both, and the Prince Regent, too, in the White Conduit fields, on which spot Mr. Goldham built his present house. Great matches in those days, as in these, cost money. Six guineas to win and four to lose was the player's fee, or five and three if they lived in town. So as every match cost some seventy pounds, over the fire-place at Lord's you would see a Subscription List for Surrey against England, or for England against Kent, as the case might be, and find notices at Brooke's and other clubs.

But what were the famed cricket Counties in these twenty years ? The glory of Kent had for a time departed. Time was when Kent could challenge England man for man, but now only with such odds as twenty-three to twelve. As to its wide extension, cricket advanced but slowly compared with recent times. Still a small circle round London would comprise all the finest players. It was not till 1820 that Norfolk, forgetting its three Elevens beaten by Lord Frederick, again played Marylebone, and though three gentlemen were given and Fuller Pilch played—then a lad of seventeen years—Norfolk lost by 417 runs, including Mr. Ward's longest score on record—278. " But he was missed," said Mr. Budd, " the easiest possible catch before he had scored thirty." Kennington Oval, perhaps, was then all docks and thistles. Still Surrey was the first cricket county, and Mr. Laurell (Robinson was his keeper ; an awful man for poachers, 6 feet 1 inch, and 16 stone, and strong in proportion), most generous of supporters, was not slow to give orders on Lord for golden guineas, when a Surrey man by catch, or innings, called forth applause. Of the same high order were Sir J. Cope of Bramshill Park and Mr. Barnett, the banker, promoter of the B. matches ; Hon. D. Kinnaird, and Mr. W. Ward, who by purchase of a lease saved Lord's from building ground ; an act of generosity in which he imitated the good old Duke of Dorset, who, said Mr. Budd, " gave the ground called the Vine, at Sevenoaks, to the use of cricketers for ever."

The good men of Surrey, in 1800, monopolised nearly all the play of England. Lord Frederick Beauclerk and Hammond were the only All England players not Surrey men.

Kent had then some civil contests—petty wars of single clans—but no county match ; and their great friend, R. Whitehead, Esq., depended on the M.C.C. for his finest games.   The game had become a profession : a science to the gentlemen, and an art or handicraft to the players ; and Farnham found in London the best market for its cricket as for its hops.   The best Kent play was displayed at Rochester, and yet more at Woolwich, but chiefly among our officers, whose bats were bought in London, not at Sevenoaks.   Games reflecting none such honour to the county as when the Earls of Thanet and of Darnley brought their own tenantry to Lord's or Dartford Brent, armed with the native willow wood of Kent.   So the Honourables H. and J. Tuffton were obliged to yield to the altered times, and play two-and-twenty men where their noble father, the Earl of Thanet, had won with eleven. " Thirteen to twenty three was the number we enjoyed," said Sparkes, " for with thirteen good men well-placed, and the bowling good, we did not want their twenty-three.   A third man on, and a forward point, or kind of middle wicket, with slow bowling, or an extra slip with fast, made a very strong field : the Kent men were sometimes regularly pounded."

In 1805 we find a curious match : the " twelve best against twenty-three next best."   Lord Frederick was the only amateur among the former ; but Barton, one of the " next best " among the latter, proved worth 100 runs !   Mr. Budd first appeared at Lords in 1808, and was among the longest scorers from the very first.

The Homerton Club also furnished an annual match : still all within the sound of Bow bells.   " To forget Homerton," said Mr. Ward, " were to ignore, Mr. Vigne, our wicket-keeper, but one of very moderate powers.   Hammond was the best we ever had.   He played till his sixtieth year ; but Browne and Osbaldeston put all wicket-keeping to the rout.   Hammond's great success was in the days of slow bowling.   John Wells and Howard were the two best fast bowlers, though Powell was very true.   Osbaldeston beat his side with byes and slips—thirty byes in the B. match." Few men could hit him before wicket ; whence the many single wicket matches he played ; but Mr. Ward put an end to his reign by finding out Browne of Brighton.   Beagley said of Browne, as the players now say of Mr. Fellows, they had no objection to him when the ground was smooth.

The Homerton Club also boasted of Mr. Ladbroke, one of the great promoters of matches, as well as the late Mr. Aislaby, always fond of the game, but all his life " too big to play "—the remark by

Lord Frederick of Mr. Ward, which, being repeated, did no little to develop the latent powers of that most efficient player.

The Montpelier Club, also, with men given, annually played Marylebone.

Lord Frederick, in 1803, gave a little variety to the matches by leading against Marylebone ten men of Leicester and Nottingham with the two Warsops. " T. Warsop," said Clarke, " was one of the best bowlers I ever knew." Clarke has also a high opinion of Lambert, from whom he learnt more of the game than from any other man.

Lambert's bowling was like Mr. Budd's, against which I have often played : a high underhand delivery, slow, but rising very high, very accurately pitched, and turning in from leg stump. " About the year 1818, Lambert and I," said Mr. Budd, " attained to a kind of round-armed delivery (described as Clarke's), by which we rose decidedly superior to all the batsmen of the day. Mr. Ward could not play it, but he headed a party against us, and our new bowling was ignored." Tom Walker and Lord Frederick were of the tediously slow school ; Lambert and Budd several degrees faster. Howard and John Wells were the fast underhand bowlers.

Lord Frederick was a very successful bowler, but was at last beat by men running into him. Sparkes mentioned another player who brought very slow bowling to perfection, and beat in the same way. Beldham thought Mr. Budd's bowling better than Lord Frederick's.

His Lordship is generally supposed to have been the best amateur of his day—an assertion I can by no means reconcile with acknowledged facts ; for Mr. Budd made the best average, though usually placed against Lambert's bowling, and playing almost exclusively in the great matches. Mr. Budd was a much more powerful hitter. Lord Frederick said, " Budd always wanted to win the game off a single ball " : Beldham observed, " if Mr. Budd would not hit so eagerly, he would be the finest player in all England." When I knew him his hitting was quite safe play.

But since Mr. Budd had the largest average in spite of his hitting, Beldham becomes a witness in his favour. Mr. Budd measured five feet ten inches, and weighed twelve stone, very clean made and powerful, with an eye singularly keen, and great natural quickness, being one of the fastest runners of his day. He stood usually at middle wicket. I never saw safer hands at a catch ; and I have seen him very quick at stumping out. But Lord Frederick could not take every part of the field ; but was always short slip,

and not one of the very best. Mr. Budd hit well with the wrist.
At Woolwich he hit a volley to long field for nine, though Parry
threw it in. He also hit out of Lord's old ground. " Lord had
said he would forfeit twenty-five guineas if any one thus proved his
ground too small : so we all crowded around Budd," said Beldham,
" and told him what he might claim. ' Well, then,' he said, ' I
claim it, and give it among the players.' But Lord was shabby and
would not pay." Mr. Budd is now in his sixty-sixth year, still I
have never seen the country Eleven that could spare him yet.

Lambert was also good at every point. In batting, he was a
bold forward player. He stood with left foot a yard in advance,
swaying his bat and body as if to attain momentum, and reaching
forward almost to where the ball must pitch.

Lambert's chief point was to take the ball at the pitch and
drive it powerfully away, and, said Mr. Budd, " to a slow bowler
his return was so quick and forcible, that his whole manner was
really intimidating to a bowler." Every one remarked how completely Lambert seemed master of the ball. Usually the bowler
appears to attack, and the batsman to defend ; but Lambert seemed
always on the attack, and the bowler at his mercy, and " hit," said
Beldham, " what no one else could meddle with."

Lord Frederick was formed on Beldham's style. Mr. Budd's
position at the wicket was much the same : the right foot placed as
usual, but the left rather behind, and nearly a yard apart, so that
instead of the upright bat and figure of Pilch, the bat was drawn
across, and the figure hung away from the wicket. This was a
mistake. Before the ball could be played Mr. Budd was too good
a player not to be up, like Pilch, and play well over his off stump.
Still Mr. Budd explained to me that this position of the left foot
was just where one naturally shifts it to have room for a cut : so
this strange attitude was supposed to favour their fine off hits.
I say Off hit because the Cut did not properly belong to either of
these players : Robinson and Saunders were the men to cut—cutting
balls clean away from the bails, though Robinson had a maimed
hand, burnt when a child : the handle of his bat was grooved to
fit his stunted fingers. Talking of his bat, the players once discovered
by measurement it was beyond the statute width, and would not
pass through the standard. So, unceremoniously, a knife was
produced, and the bat reduced to rather its just than fair proportions.
" Well," said Robinson, " I'll pay you off for spoiling my bat " ;
and sure enough he did, hitting tremendously, and making one of
his largest innings, which were often near a hundred runs.

Figure 11. M.C.C. *v.* Kent at Lord's, 1793. A game played on 20th June 'between the Earls of Winchelsea and Darnley for 1000 guineas'.

Figure 12. A local game in progress at Warfield Church,

During these twenty years, Hampshire, like Kent, had lost its renown, but simply because Hambledon was now no more ; nor did Surrey and Hampshire any longer count as one. To confirm our assertion that Farnham produced the players—for in 1808, Surrey had played and beat England three times in one season, and from 1820 to 1825 Godalming is mentioned as the most powerful antagonist : but whether called Godalming or Surrey, we must not forget that the locality is the same—we observe, that in 1821, M.C.C. plays " The Three Parishes," namely, Godalming, Farnham, and Hartley Row, which parishes, after rearing the finest contemporaries of Beldham, then boasted a later race of players in Flavel, Searle, Howard, Thumwood, Mathews.

" About this time (July 23, 1821)," said Beldham, " we played the Coronation Match : ' M.C.C. against the Players of England.' We scored 278 and only six wickets down, when the game was given up. I was hurt and could not run my notches ; still James Bland, and the other Legs, begged of me to take pains, for it was no sporting match, ' any odds and no takers ' ; and they wanted to shame the gentlemen against wasting their (the Legs') time in the same way another time."

But the day for Hampshire, as for Kent, was doomed to shine again. Fennex, Small, the Walkers, J. Wells and Hammond, in time drop off from Surrey—and about the same time, 1815, Caldecourt, Holloway, Beagley, Thumwood, Shearman, Howard, Mr. Ward, and Mr. Knight, restore the balance of power for Hants, as afterwards, Broadbridge and Lillywhite for Sussex.

" In 1817, we went," said Mr. Budd, " with Osbaldestone to play twenty-two of Nottingham. In that match Clarke played. In common with others I lost my money, and was greatly disappointed at the termination. One paid player was accused of selling, and never employed after. The concourse of people was very great : these were the days of the Luddites (rioters), and the magistrates warned us, that unless we would stop our game at seven o'clock, they could not answer for keeping the peace. At seven o'clock we stopped, and simultaneously the thousands who lined the ground began to close in upon us. Lord Frederick lost nerve and was very much alarmed ; but I said they didn't want to hurt us. " No ; they simply came to have a look at the eleven men who ventured to play two for one." His Lordship broke his finger, and batting, with one hand, scored only eleven runs. Nine men, the largest number perhaps on record, are recorded as ' caught by Budd.'"

Just before the establishment of Mr. Will's roundhand bowling, as if to prepare the way, Ashby came forth with an unusual bias, but no great pace. Sparkes bowled in the same style ; as also Matthews and Mr. Jenner somewhat later. Still the batsmen were full as powerful as ever, reckoning Saunders, Searle, Beagley, Messrs. Ward, Kingscote, Knight ; Suffolk became very strong with Pilch, the Messrs. Blake, and others, of the famous Bury Club ; while Slater, Lillywhite, King, and the Broadbridges, raised the name of Midhurst and of Sussex.

Against such batsmen every variety of underhand delivery failed to maintain the balance of the game, till J. Broadbridge and Lillywhite after many protests and discussions, succeeded in establishing what long was called " the Sussex bowling."

" About 1820," said Mr. Budd, " at our anniversary dinner (three-guinea tickets) at the Clarendon, Mr. Ward asked me if I had said I would play any man in England at single wicket, without fieldsmen. An affirmative produced a match p. p. for fifty guineas. On the day appointed Mr. Brand proved my opponent. He was a fast bowler. I went in first, and, scoring seventy runs with some severe blows on the legs—nankeen knees and silk stockings, and no pads in those days—I consulted a friend and knocked down my own wicket, lest the match should last to the morrow and I be unable to play. Mr. Brand was out without a run ! I went in again, and making up the 70 to 100, I once more knocked down my own wicket, and once more my opponent failed to score ! !

The flag was flying—the signal of a great match—and a large concourse were assembled, and, considering Mr. Ward, a good judge, made the match, this is probably the most hollow beat on record.

Osbaldestone's victory was even more satisfactory. Lord Frederick with Beldham made a p. p. match with Osbalestone and Lambert. " On the day named," said Budd, " I went to Lord Frederick, representing my friend was too ill to stand, and asking him to put off the match. " No ; play or pay," said his Lordship, quite inexorable. " Never mind," said Osbaldestone, " I won't forfeit : Lambert may beat them both, and if he does the fifty guineas shall be his." I asked Lambert how he felt. " Why," said he, " they are anything but safe." His Lordship wouldn't hear of it. " Nonsense," he said, " you can't mean it." " Yes ; play or pay, my Lord, we are in earnest, and shall claim the stakes ! " and in fact Lambert did beat them both. For to play such a man when on his mettle was rather discouraging, and " he did make desperate exertion " : said Beldham, " once he rushed up after the ball, and Lord Frederick was caught so near his bat that he lost his temper, and said it was not fair play. Of course all hearts were with Lambert."

" Osbaldestone's mother sat by in her carriage, and enjoyed the match, and then," said Beldham, " Lambert was called to the carriage and bore away a paper parcel : some said it was a gold watch—some, bank notes. Trust Lambert to keep his own secrets. We were all curious, but no one every knew."

CHAPTER VI.

A DARK CHAPTER IN THE HISTORY OF CRICKET

THE lovers of cricket may congratulate themselves at the present day that matches are made at cricket, as at chess, rather for love and the honour of victory than for money.

It is now many years since Lord's was frequented by men with book and pencil, betting as openly and professionally as in the ring at Epsom, and ready to deal in the odds with any and every person of speculative propensities. Far less satisfactory was the state of things with which Lord F. Beauclerk and Mr. Ward had to contend, to say nothing of the earlier days of the Earl of Winchelsea and Sir Horace Mann. As to the latter period " Old Nyren " bewails its evil doings. He speaks of one who had " the trouble of proving himself a rogue," and also of " the legs at Marylebone," who tried, for once in vain, to corrupt some primitive specimens of Hambledon innocence. He says, also, the grand matches of his day were always made for 500 *l.* a side. Add to this the fact that the bets were in proportion, that Jim and Joe Bland of turf notoriety, Dick Whitlom of Covent Garden, Simpson, a gaming-house keeper, and Toll of Isher, as regularly attended at a match as Crockford and Gully at Epsom and Ascot ; and the idea that all the Surrey and Hampshire rustics should either want or resist strong temptations to sell is not to be entertained for a moment. The constant habit of betting will take the honesty out of any man. A half-crown sweepstakes or betting such odds as lady's long kids to gentleman's short ditto is all very fair sport ; but if a man after years of high betting can still preserve the fine edge and tone of honest feeling he is indeed a wonder. To bet on a certainty all admit is swindling. If so, to bet where you feel it a certainty must be very bad moral practice.

" If gentlemen wanted to bet," said Beldham, " just under the pavilion sat men ready with money down to give and take the current odds, and by far the best men to bet with, because if they lost it was all in the way of business : they paid their money and did not grumble. Still they had all sorts of tricks to make their betting safe. " One artifice," said Mr. Ward, " was to keep a player out of the way by a false report that his wife was dead." Then these men would come down to the Green Man and Still and drink with us, and always said that those who backed us, or

" the nobs," as they called them, sold the matches ; and so, sir, as you are going the round beating up the quarters of the old players, you will find some to persuade you this is true. But don't believe it. That any gentleman in my day ever put himself into the power of these blacklegs by selling matches, I can't credit. Still one day I thought I would try how far these tales were true. So, going down into Kent with " one of high degree," he said to me, " Will, if this match is won, I lose a hundred pounds." " Well," said I, " my Lord, you and I could order that." He smiled as if nothing were meant, and talked of something else ; and, as luck would have it, he and I were in together, and brought up the score between us, though every run seemed to me like " a guinea out of his Lordship's pocket."

In those days foot races were very common. Lord Frederick and Mr. Budd were first-rate runners, and bets were freely laid. So one day old Fennex laid a trap for the gentlemen : he brought up to act the part of some silly conceited youngster, with his pockets full of money, a first-rate runner out of Hertfordshire. This soft young gentleman ran a match or two with some known third-rate men, and seemed to win by a neck, and no pace to spare. Then he calls out, " I'll run any man on the ground for 25 *l.*, money down." A match was quickly made, and money laid on pretty thick on Fennex's account. Some said, " Too bad to win of such a green young fellow " ; others said, " He's old enough—serve him right." So the laugh was finely against those who were taken in ; " the green one " ran away like a hare !

" You see, sir," said one fine old man, with brilliant eye and quickness of movement, that showed his right hand had not yet forgot its cunning, " matches were bought, and matches were sold, and gentlemen who meant honestly lost large sums of money, till the rogues beat themselves at last. They overdid it ; they spoilt their own trade ; and, as I told one of them, a knave and a fool makes a bad partnership : so, you and yourself will never prosper. Well, surely there was robbery enough, and not a few of the great players earned money to their own disgrace ; but, if you'll believe me, there was not half the selling there was said to be. Yes, I can guess, sir, much as you have been talking to all the old players over this good stuff (pointing to the brandy and water I had provided), no doubt you have heard that B. sold as bad as the rest. I'll tell the truth : one match up the country I did sell—a match made by Mr. Osbaldstone at Nottingham. I had been sold out of a match just before, and lost 10 *l.*, and happening to hear it I joined

two others of our eleven to sell, and get back my money. I won
10 *l.* exactly, and of this roguery no one ever suspected me ; but
many was the time I have been blamed for selling when as innocent
as a babe.   In those days when so much money was on the matches,
every man who lost his money would blame some one.   Then if
A. missed a catch, or B. made no runs—and where's the player
whose hand is always in ?—that man was called a rogue directly.
So when a man was doomed to lose his character and bear all the
smart, there was the more temptation to do like others, and after
" the Kicks " to come in for " the halfpence."   But I am an old
man now, and heartily sorry I have been ever since, because, but
for that Nottingham match, I could have said with a clear conscience
to a gentleman like you, that all that was said was false, and I
never sold a match in my life ; but now I can't.   But if I had fifty
sons I would never put one of them, for all the games in the world,
in the way of the roguery that I have witnessed.   The temptation
really was very great—too great by far for any poor man to be
exposed to—no richer than ten shillings a week, let alone harvest
time.   I never told you the way I first was brought to London.   I
was a lad of eighteen at this Hampshire village, and Lord Winchelsea had seen us play among ourselves, and watched the match
with the Hambledon Club on Broad-halfpenny, when I scored
forty-three against David Harris, and ever so many of the runs
against David's bowling, and no one ever could manage David
before.   So, next year, in the month of March, I was down in the
meadows, when a gentleman came across the field with Farmer
Hilton, and thought I, all in a minute, now this is something about
cricket.   Well, at last it was settled I was to play Hampshire against
England, at London, in White Conduit-Fields ground, in the month
of June.   For three months I did nothing but think about that
match.   Tom Walker was to travel up from this county, and I
agreed to go with him, and found myself at last with a merry
company of cricketers, all old men, whose names I had ever heard
as foremost in the game—met together, drinking, card playing,
betting, and singing at the Green Man (that was the great cricketer's
house), in Oxford Street—no man without his wine, I assure you,
and such suppers as three guineas a game to lose, and five to win
(that was then the pay for players) could never pay for long.   To
go to London by a waggon, earn five guineas three or four times
told, and come back with half the money in your pocket to the
plough again, was all very well talking.   You know what young
folk are, sir, when they get together : mischief brews stronger in

large quantities : so many spent all their earnings, and were soon glad to make more money some other way. Hundreds of pounds were bet upon the great matches, and other wagers laid on the scores of the finest players, and that too by men who had a book for every race, and every match in the sporting world ; men who lived by gambling ; and as to honesty, gambling and honesty don't often go together. What was easier, then, than for such sharp gentlemen to mix with the players, take advantage of their diffi- culties, and say, your backers, my Lord this, and the Duke of that, sell matches and over-rule all your good play, so why shouldn't you have a share of the plunder ? That was their constant argument. Serve them as they serve you. You have heard of Jim Bland, the turfsman, and his brother Joe—two nice boys. When Jemmy Dawson was hanged for poisoning the horse, the Blands never felt safe till the rope was round Dawson's neck, and, to keep him quiet, persuaded him to the last hour that they dared not hang him ; and a certain nobleman had a reprieve in his pocket. Well, one day in April, Joe Bland found me out in this parish, and tried his game on with me. ' You may make a fortune,' he said, ' if you will listen to me : so much for the match with Surrey, and so much more for the Kent match—' ' Stop,' said I : ' Mr. Bland, you talk too fast ; I am rather too old for this trick ; you never buy the same man but once : if their lordships ever sold at all, you would peach upon them if ever after they dared to win. You'll try me once, and then you'll have me in line like him of the mill last year.' No, Sir, a man was a slave when once he sold to these folk : fool and knave aye go together. Still they found fools enough for their purpose ; but rogues can never trust each other. One day a sad quarrel arose between two of them ; that opened the gentlemen's eyes too wide to close again to these practices. Two very big rogues at Lord's fell a quarrelling, and blows were given ; a crowd drew round, and the gentlemen ordered them both into the pavilion. When the one began, ' you had 20l. to lose the Kent match, bowling leg long hops and missing catches.' ' And you were paid to lose at Swaffham.'—' Why did that game with Surrey turn about— three runs to get, and you didn't make them ? ' Angry words come out fast, and when they are circumstantial and square with previous suspicions, they are proofs as strong as holy writ. In one single- wicket match," he continued, " and those were always great matches for the sporting men, because usually you had first-rate men on each side, and their merits known ; dishonesty was as plain as this : just as a player was coming in (John B. will confess this if you talk of the match) he said to me, ' you'll let me score five or six, for appearances, won't you, for I am not going to make many if I can ? ' ' Yes,' I said, ' you rogue, you shall if I can not help it.' But when a game was all but won, and the odds heavy, and all one way, it was cruel to see how the fortune of the day then would change about. In that Kent match, you can turn to it in your book (Bentley's scores), played 28th July, 1807, on Pennenden Heath, I and Lord Frederick had scored sixty-one, and thirty remained to win, and six of the best men in England went out for eleven runs. Well, sir, I lost some money by that match, and as seven of us were walking homewards to meet a coach, a gentleman who had backed the match drove by and said, ' Jump up, my boys, we have all lost together. I need not mind if I hire a pair of horses extra next town, for I have lost money enough to pay for twenty pair or more.' Well, thought I, as I rode along, you have rogues enough in your carriage now, if the truth were told, I'll answer for it ; and one of them let out the secret some ten years after. But, sir, I can't help laughing when I tell you, once there was a single-wicket match played at Lord's, and a man on each side was paid to lose. One was bowler, and the other batsman, when the game came to a near point. I knew their politics, the rascals, and saw in a minute how things stood ; and how I did laugh to be sure ; for seven balls together, one would not bowl straight, and the other would not hit ; but at last a straight ball must come, and down went the wicket."

From other information received, I could tell this veteran that, even in his much-repented Nottingham match, his was not the only side that had men resolved to lose. The match was sold for Nottingham too, and that with less success, for Nottingham won ; an event the less difficult to accomplish, as Lord Frederick Beauclerk broke a finger in an attempt to stop a designed and wilful overthrow ! and played the second innings with one hand.

It is true, Clarke, who played in the match, thought all was fair : still, he admits, he heard one Nottingham man accused on the field by his own side of foul play. This confirms the evidence of the Rev. C. W., no slight authority on Nottingham matches, who said he was cautioned before the match that all would not be fair.

" This practice of selling matches," said Beldham, " produced strange things sometimes. Once, I remember, England was playing Surrey, and, in my judgment, Surrey had the best side ; still I found the Legs were betting seven to four against Surrey ! This time they were done ; for they betted on the belief that some Surrey men had sold the match, but Surrey played to win.

Crockford used to be seen about Lord's, and Mr. Gully also occasionally, but only for society of sporting men : they did not understand the game, and I never saw them bet. Mr. Gully was often talking to me about the game for one season ; but I could never put any sense into him ! He knew plenty about fighting, and afterwards of horse-racing ; but a man cannot learn the odds of cricket unless he is something of a player."

CHAPTER IX.

BOWLING—AN HOUR WITH "OLD CLARKE"

IN cricket wisdom Clarke is truly " Old " : what he has learnt from anybody, he learnt from Lambert. But he is a man who thinks for himself, and knows men and manners. " I beg your pardon, sir," he one day said to a gentleman taking guard, " but ain't you Harrow ? "—" then we shan't want a man down there," he said, addressing a fieldsman ; " stand for the ' Harrow drive,' between point and middle wicket."

The time to see Clarke is the morning of a match. While others are practising, he walks round with his hands under the flaps of his coat, reconnoitring his adversaries' wicket.

" Before you bowl to a man, it is worth something to know what is running in his head. That gentleman," he will say, " is too fast on his feet, so, as good as ready money to me : if he doesn't hit he can't score ; if he does I shall have him."

Going a little further, he sees a man lobbing to another, who is practising stepping in. " There, sir, is ' practising to play Clarke,' that is very plain ; and a nice mess, you will see, he will make of it. Ah ! my friend, if you do go in at all, you must go in further than that, or my twist will beat you ; and going in to swipe round, eh ! Learn to run me down with a straight bat, and I will say something to you. But that wouldn't score quite fast enough for your notions. Going into hit round is a tempting of Providence."

" There, that man is pure stupid : alter the pace and height with a dropping ball, and I shall have no trouble with him. They think, sir, it is nothing but ' Clarke's vexatious pace ' : they know nothing about the curves. With fast bowling, you cannot have half my variety ; and when you have found out the weak point, where's the fast bowler that can give the exact ball to hit it ? There is often no more head-work in fast bowling than there is in the catapult : without head-work I should be hit out of the field."

" A man is never more taken aback than when he prepares for one ball, and I bowl him the contrary one : there was Mr. Nameless, the first time he came to Nottingham, full of fancies about playing me. The first ball he walked some yards out to meet me, and I pitched over his head, so near his wicket, that, thought I, that bird won't fight again. Next ball he was a little cunning, and made a feint of coming out, meaning, as I guessed, to stand back for a long hop ; so I pitched right up to him ; and he was so bent upon cutting me away, that he hit his own wicket down ! "

Clarke is represented as bowling two balls of different lengths ; but the increased height of the shorter pitched ball, by a natural ocular delusion, makes it appear as far pitched as the other. If the batsman is deceived in playing at both balls by the same forward play, he endangers his wicket. " See, there," continues Clarke, " that gentleman's is a dodge certainly, but not a new one either. He does step in it is true ; but while hitting at the ball, he is so anxious about getting back again, that his position has all the danger of stepping in, and none of its advantages."

" Then there is Mr. . .," naming a great man struggling with adversity. " He gives a jump up off his feet, and thinks he is stepping in, but comes flump down just where he was before."

" Pilch plays me better than any one. But he knows better than to step in to every ball, or to stand fast every ball. He plays steadily, and discriminates, waiting till I give him a chance, and then makes the most of it."

Bowling consists of two parts : there is the mechanical part, and the intellectual part. First you want the hand to pitch where you please and then the head to know where to pitch, according to the player.

CHAPTER OF ACCIDENTS—MISCELLANEOUS

Let any man of common judgment see the velocity with which the ball flies from the bats of first-rate players, and how near the fieldsmen stand to the hitter ; and then let him feel and weigh a ball in his hand, and he would naturally expect to hear that every public cricket ground was in near connection with some casualty hospital, so deceptive is a priori reasoning. William Beldham saw as much of cricket as any other man in England from the year 1780 to about 1820. Mr. E. H. Budd and Caldecourt are the best of the chroniclers from the days of Beldham down to George Parr. Yet neither of these worthies could remember any injury at cricket, that would at all compare with the " moving accidents of flood and field " that have thinned the ranks of Nimrod, Hawker, or Isaac Walton. Fatal accidents in any legitimate game of cricket there have been none. There is a rumour of a boy at school, about fifteen years since, and another boy about twenty-five years ago, being severally

killed by a blow on the head with a ball : a dirty boy also of
Salisbury town, in 1826, having a bad habit of pocketing the balls
of the pupils of Dr. Ratcliffe's school, was hit rather hard on the
head with a brass-tipped middle stump, and, by a strange coinci-
dence, died of " excess of passion," as the jury found a few hours
after. A man fell over the stumps but a short time since, and died
of the injury sustained in the leg. But all this proves little as to
the danger of the game.

The most likely source of serious injury, and one which has
caused alarm and shaken the nerves of not a few, is when a hitter,
which is most rare, returns the ball with all his force, straight back
to the bowler. Caldecourt and the Rev. C. Wordsworth, than
whom a more free and forcible hitter to every point of the field
was never bred at Harrow nor played at Winchester, severally and
separately remarked in my hearing that they had shuddered at
cricket once, each in the same position, and each from the same
hitter. Each had a ball hit back to him by that powerful hitter
Colonel Kingscote, which whizzed in defiance of hand or eye, most
dangerously by. A similar hit we described from Hammond
stepping in at the pitch, just missed Lord F. Beauclerk's head, and
spoiled his nerve for bowling ever after. But what if these several
balls had really hit ? who knows whether the skull might not have
stood the shock, as in a case which I witnessed in Oxford in 1835 ;
when one Richard Blucher, a Cowley bowler, was hit on the head
by a clean half volley, from the bat of Henry Daubeney—than
whom few Wykehamists used (*fuit !*) to hit with better eye or
stronger arm. Still " Richard was himself again," for we saw a
man with his head tied up, bowling at shillings the very next day.
Some skulls stand a great deal. Witness the sprigs of Shillelah in
Donybrooke fair ; still most indubitably tender in the face ; as
also—which *horresco referens* ; but here let me tell wicket keepers,
and longstops especially, that a cricket jacket made long and full,
with pockets to hold a handkerchief sufficiently in front, is a pre-
caution not to be despised, though " the race of inventive men "
have also devised a cross-bar India rubber guard, aptly described
in Achilles' threat to Thersites, in the first Iliad ; though I can
truly say, like Bob Acres at the sight of the doctor's implements,
the sight of them " takes away my fighting stomach."

The most alarming accident I ever saw occurred in one of the
many matches played by the Lansdown Club against Mr. E. H.
Budd's Eleven, at Purton, in 1835. Two of the Lansdown players
were running between wickets ; and good Mr. Prout—*immani*

corpore—was standing mid way, and hiding each from the other. Both rushing the same side of him, and one with his bat most dangerously extended, the point of which met his partner under the chin, forced back his head as if his neck were broken, and dashed him senseless to the ground. Never shall I forget the shudder and the chill of every heart, till poor Price—for he it was, was lifted up—gradually evinced returning consciousness; and at length, when all was explained, he smiled, amidst his bewilderment, with his usual good-nature, on his unlucky friend. A surgeon, who witnessed the collision, feared he was dead, and said, afterwards, that with less powerful muscles (for he had a neck like a bull-dog) he never could have stood the shock. Price told me next day that he felt as if a little more and he never should have raised his head again.

And what Wykehamist of 1820-30 does not remember R... Price? or what Fellow of New College down to 1847, when
    "*Multis ille bonis flebilis occidit,*"
has not enjoyed his merriment in the Common Room or his play on Bullingdon and Cowley Marsh? His were the safest hands and most effective fielding ever seen. To attempt the one run from a cover hit when Price was there, or to give the sight of one stump to shy at, with a wicket lost. When his friend, F. B. Wright, or any one he could trust, was at the wicket, well backed up, the ball by the fine old Wykehamist action was up and in with such speed and precision as I have hardly seen equalled and never exceeded. When he came to Lord's, in 1825, with that Wykehamist Eleven which Mr. Ward so long remembered with delight, their play was unknown and the bets on their opponents; but when once Price was seen practising at a single stump, his Eleven became the favourites immediately, for he was one of the straightest of all fast bowlers; and I have heard experienced batsmen say, 'We don't care for his underhand bowling, only it is so straight we could take no liberties, and the first we missed was Out.' I never envied any man his sight and nerve like Price—the coolest practitioner you ever saw; he always looked bright, though others blue: you had only to look at his sharp grey eyes, and you could at once account for the fact that one stump to shy at, a rook for a single bullet, or the ripple of a trout in a bushey stream, was so much fun for R. Price.

Some of the most painful accidents have been of the same kind— from collision; therefore I never blame a man who, as the ball soars high in air, and the captain of his side does not (as he ought if he can) call out " Johnson has it ! " stops short, for fear of three spikes in his instep, or the buttons of his neighbour's jacket forcibly coinciding with his own. Still these are hardly the dangers of cricket : men may run their heads together in the street.

The principal injuries sustained are in the fingers ; though I did once know a gentleman who played in spectacles ; and seeing two balls in the air, caught at the shadow, and nearly had the substance in his face. The old players, in the days of under-hand bowling, played without gloves ; and Bennett assured me he had seen Tom Walker, before advancing civilisation made man tender, rub his bleeding fingers in the dust. The old players could show finger-joints of most ungenteel dimensions ; and no wonder, for a finger has been broken even through tubular india rubber. Still, with a good pair of cricket gloves no man need think much about his fingers ; albeit flesh will blacken, joints will grow too large for the accustomed ring, and finger-nails will come off. A spinning ball is the most mischievous ; and when there is spin and pace too, as with a ball from Mr. Fellows, which you can hear humming like a top, the danger is too great for mere amusement ; for when, as in the Players' Match of 1849, Hillyer plays a bowler a foot away from his stumps, and Pilch cannot face him, which is true when Mr. Fellows bowls on any but the smoothest ground, why then we will not say that anything that hardest of hitters and thorough cricketer does is not cricket, but certainly it's anything but *play*.

Some of the worst injuries of the hands occur rather in fielding than in batting. A fine player of the Kent Eleven, about three years ago, so far injured his thumb that the middle joint was removed, and he has rarely played since. Another of the best players of his day broke a bone in his hand in putting down a wicket : but, strangest of all, I saw a Christchurch man at Oxford fielding Cover split up his hand an inch in length between his second and third fingers ; but a celebrated university doctor of that day—y-clept " *Mercurialium custos virorum* "—made all well in a few weeks, and in the same season a fine young fellow had a finger nail completely taken off in catching a ball.

Add to all these chances of war, the many balls that are flying at the same time at Lord's and the University, and other much frequented grounds, on a practising day. At Oxford you may see, any day in the summer, on Cowley Marsh, two rows of six wickets each, facing each other, with a space of about sixty yards between each row, and ten between each wicket. Then you have twelve bowlers, *dos a dos*, and as many hitters—making twelve balls and twenty-four men, all in danger's way at once, besides bystanders.

The most any one of these bowlers can do is to look out for the balls of his own set ; whether hit or not by a ball from behind is very much a matter of chance. A ball from the opposite row once touched my hair. The wonder is, that twelve balls should be flying in a small space for nearly every day, yet I never heard of any man being hit in the face—a fact the more remarkable because there was usually free hitting and loose bowling. One day, at Lord's, just before the match bell rung after dinner, I saw one of the hardest hitters in the M.C.C. actually trying how hard he could drive among the various clusters of six-penny amateurs, every man thinking it fun, and no one dangerous. Certainly, body-blows from a ball no man regards ; and as to legs, the calves, as an Irishman remarked, save the shins behind, and the hands before. An elderly gentleman cannot stand a bruise so well—matter forms or bone exfoliates. But then, an elderly gentleman, bearing an inverse ratio in all things to him who calls him ' governor,' is the most careful thing in nature ; while young blood circulates too fast to be overtaken by half the ills that flesh is heir to.

A well known Wykehamist player of R. Price's standing, was lately playing as wicket keeper, and seeing the batsman going to hit off, ran almost to the place of a near Point ; the hit, tremendously hard, glanced off from his forehead—he called out "Catch it," and it was caught by bowler ! He was not hurt—not even marked by the ball.

Four was scored at Beckenham, 1850, by a hit that bounded off point's head ; but the player suffered much in this instance.

A spot under the window of the tavern at Lord's was marked as the evidence of a famous hit by Mr. Budd, and when I played, Oxford v. Cambridge in 1836, a son of Lord F. Beauclerk hitting above that spot elicited the observation from the old players. Beagley hit a ball from his Lordship over a bank 120 yards. Freemantle's famous hit was 130 yards in the air. Freemantle's bail was once hit up and fell back on the stump : Not out. A similar thing was witnessed by a friend on the Westminster Ground. " One hot day," said Bailey, " I saw a new stump bowled out of the perpendicular, but the bail stuck in the groove from the melting of the varnish in the sun, and the batsman continued his innings." I have seen Mr. Kirwan hit a bail thirty yards. A bail has flown forty yards.

I once chopped hard down upon a shooter, and the ball went a foot away from my bat straight forward towards the bowler, and then, by its rotary motion, returned in the same straight line exactly, like the " draw-back stroke " at billiards, and shook the bail off.

At a match played at Cambridge, a lost ball was found so firmly fixed on the point of a broken glass bottle in an ivied wall, that a new ball was necessary to continue the game.

Among remarkable games of cricket, are games on the ice—as on Christchurch meadow, Oxford, in 1849, and other places. The one-armed and one-legged pensioners of Greenwich and Chelsea is an oft-repeated match.

Mr. Trumper and his dog challenged and beat two players at single wicket in 1825, on Harefield common, near Rickmansworth.

Matches of much interest have been played between members of the same family and some other club. Besides " the Twelve Cæsars," the three Messrs. Walker and the Messrs. Ridding have proved how cricket may run in a family, not to forget three of the House of Verulam, one of whom, especially, plays in as fine a style as any of the present day ; and as to hard hitting, a second has, I am informed, hit over the Tennis Court.

Pugilists have rarely been cricket players. " We used to see the fighting men," said Beldham, " playing skittles about the ground, but there were no players among them." Ned O'Neal was a pretty good player, and we did hear that Bendigo challenged George Parr ; but no one imputed it to any distrust in his own play that Parr declined that honour. Certainly no man was ever famous both in the ring and at Lord's.

In the famous Nottingham match, 1817, Bentley, on the All England side, was playing well, when he was given " run out," having run round his ground. " Why," said Beldham, " he had been home long enough to take a pinch of snuff." They changed the umpire ; but the blunder lost the match.

" Spiked shoes," said Beldham, " were not in use in my country. Never saw them till I went to Hambledon." " Robinson began with spikes of a monstrous length," said old Mr. Moreton, the dramatist, " on one foot." " The first notion of a leg guard I ever saw," said an old player, " was Robinson's : he put together two thin boards, angle-wise, on his right shin : the ball would go off it as clean as off the bat, but made a precious deal more noise : but it was laughed at—did not last long. Robinson burnt some of his fingers off when a child, and had the handle of his bat cut to suit the stumps. Still, he was a fine hitter.

Barton mentioned to me a one armed man who used a short bat in his right hand so well as to make a fair average score.

Sawdust.—Beldham, Robinson, and Lambert, played Bennett, Fennex, and Lord F. Beauclerk, a notable single wicket match at

Figure 13. From W. H. Pyne's *Microcosm*, 1808.

Figure 14. Headpiece from the 'Laws of the Noble Game of Cricket, as revised by the Club at St Mary-le-bone', 1809.

Lord's, 27th June, 1806. Lord Frederick's last innings was winning the game, and no chance of getting him out. His Lordship had then lately introduced sawdust when the ground was wet. Beldham, unseen, took up a lump of wet dirt and sawdust and stuck it on the ball, which, pitching favourably, made an extraordinary twist, and took the wicket. This I heard separately from Beldham, Bennett, and also Fennex, who used to mention it as among the wonders of his long life.

As to *Long Scores*, above one hundred in an innings rather lessens than adds to the interest of a game.

The greatest number recorded, with overhand bowling, was in M.C.C. *v.* Sussex, at Brighton, about 1842 ; the four innings averaged 207 each. In 1815, Epsom *v.* Middlesex, at Lord's, scored first innings, 476. Sussex *v.* Epsom, in 1817, scored 445 in one innings. Mr. Ward's great innings was 278, in M.C.C. *v.* Norfolk, 24th July, 1820, but with underhand bowling. Mr. Mynn's great innings at Leicester was in North *v.* South in 1836. South winning by 218 runs. Mr. Mynn 21 (not out) and 125 (not out) and against Redgate's bowling. Wisden, Parr, and Pilch, have scored above 100 runs in one innings against good bowling. Wisden once bowled ten wickets in one innings ; Mr. Kirwan has done the same thing.

Mr. Marcon, at Beckenham, 1850, bowled four men in four successive balls. The Lansdown Club, in 1850, put the West Gloucestershire Club out for six runs, and of these only two were scored by hits—so ten ciphers ! Eleven men last year (1850) were out for a run each ; Mr. Felix being one. Mr. G. Yonge, playing against the Etonians, put a whole side out for six runs. A friend, playing the Shepton Mallet Club, put his adversaries in second innings for seven runs to tie, and got all out for five ! In a famous Wykehamist match all depended on an outsider's making two runs : he made a hard hit. When in the moment of exultation, " Cut away, you young sinner," said a big fellow ; when lo ! down he laid his bat, and cut away to the tent ; while the other side, amidst screams of laughter at the mistake, put down the wicket and won the match.

In a match at Oxford, in 1835, I saw the two last wickets score 110 runs ; and in an I.Z. match at Leamington, the last wickets scored 80.

As to *Hard Hitting.* " One of the longest hits in air of modern days," writes a friend, " was made at Slimley about three years since by Mr. Fellows, confessedly one of the hardest of all hitters.

The same gentleman, in practice on the Leicester ground, hit, clean over the poplars, one hundred long paces from the wicket : the distance from bat to pitch of ball may be fairly stated as 140 yards. This was a longer hit, I think, than that at Slimley, which every one wondered at, though the former was off slow lobs in practice ; the latter in a match. Mr. Fellows also made so high a hit over the bowler's (Wisden's) head, that the second run was finished as the ball returned to earth ! He was afterwards caught by Armitage, Long-field On, when half through the second run. I have also seen, I think, Mr. G. Barker, of Trinity, hit a nine on Parker's Piece. It took three average throwers to throw it up. Mr. Bastard, of Trinity, hit a ten on the same ground. Sir F. Heygate, this year, hit an eight at Leicester." When Mr. Budd hit a nine at Woolwich, it proved a tie match : an eight would have lost the game. Practise clean hitting, correct position, and judgment of lengths with free arm, and the ball is sure to go far enough. The habit of hitting at a ball oscillating from a slanting pole will greatly improve any unpractised hitter. The drummer boys practise the use of the cat on a dummy. The use of the bat, by a kind of " chamber practice " mentioned, may furnish us an exercise as good as dumb bells, and far more interesting. A soft ball will answer the purpose, pierced and threaded on a string.

The most vexatious of all stupid things was done by James Broadbridge, in Sussex v. England, at Brighton, in 1827, one of the trial matches which excited such interest in the early days of over hand bowling. " We went in for 120 to win," said our good friend, Captain Cheslyn, " Now," I said, " my boys, let every man resolve on a steady game and the match is ours ; when, almost at the first set off, that stupid fellow Jim threw his bat a couple of yards at a ball too wide to reach, and Mr. Ward caught him at point ! The loss of this one man's innings was not all, for the men went in disgusted ; the quicksilver was up with the other side, and down with us, and the match was lost by twenty-four runs." But, though stupid in this instance, Broadbridge was one of the most artful dodgers that ever handled a ball. And once he practised for some match till he appeared to all the bowlers about Lord's to have reduced batting to a certainty : but when the time came, amidst the most sanguine expectations of his friends, he made no runs.

Mr. A. Bass reminds me that I have said little about generalship, a point in which I well might profit by his long experience.

I agree with Mr. Bass that his old preceptor George Owston's aim is of the greatest importance—namely, to keep his man in good humour and good spirits.

The first thing the manager has to do is to choose his Eleven ; and we have already hinted that fielding rather than batting is the qualification. A good field is sure to save runs, though the best batsman may not make any. When all are agreed on the bowlers, I would leave the bowlers to select such men as they can trust. Then in their secret conclave you will hear such principles of selection as these : " King must be point, Chatterton we cannot afford to put cover unless you can ensure Wenman to keep wicket ; Good must be longstop : his left hand saves so many draws ; and I have not nerve to attack the leg stump as I ought to with any other man. We shall have three men at least against us whom we cannot reckon on bowling out ; so if at the short slip we have a Hillyer, and at leg such a man as Coates of Sheffield, we may pick these men up pretty easily." " But as to Sir Wormwood Scrubbs, old Sloley vows he shall never get any more pine apples and champagne for the ladies' days if we don't have him, and he is about our sixth bat." " Can't be helped, for, what with his cigar and his bad temper, he will put us all wrong ; besides, we must have John Gingerley, whose only fault is chaffing, and these two men will never do together : then for middle wicket we have Young George." " Why, Edwards is quite as safe." " Yes, but not half as tractable. I would never bowl without George if I could have him ; his eye is always on me, and he will shift his place for every ball in the over, if I wish it. A handy man to put about in a moment just where you want him, is worth a great deal to a bowler."

" Then you leave out Kingsmill, Barker, and Cotesworth ? Why, they can score better than most of the tail of the Eleven ! "

" Yes ; on practising days, with loose play, but, with good men against them, what difference can there be between two men, when the first ripping ball levels both alike ? "

When taking the field, good humour and confidence, is the thing. A general who expects everything smooth, in dealing with ten fallible fellow creatures, should be at once dismissed the service : he must always have some man he had rather change as Virgil says of the bees—

Semper erunt quarum mutari corpora malis ;

but if you can have some four safe players—

Quatuor eximios præstanti corpore—

join your influence with theirs, and lead them while you seem to

consult them, and so keep up an appearance of working harmoni-
ously together. Obviously two bowlers of different pace, like Clarke
and Wisden, work well together, as also a left-handed and right-
handed batsman, like Felix and Pilch, whom we have seen run up
a hundred runs faster than ever before or since.

Nunc dextra ingeminans iclus, nunc ille sinistra.

Never put in all your best men at first, and leave " a tail " to
follow : many a game has been lost in this manner, for men lose
confidence when all the best are out : add to this most men play
better for the encouragement that a good player often gives. And
take care that you put good judges of a run in together. A good
runner starts intuitively and by habit, where a bad judge, seeing no
chance, hesitates and runs him out. If a good off hitter and a good
leg hitter are in together, the same field that checks the one will
give an opening to the other.

Frequent change of bowlers, where two men are making runs,
is good : but do not change good bowling for inferior, till it is hit,
unless you know your batsman is a dangerous man, only waiting
till his eyes are open.

With a fine forward player, a near middle wicket or forward
point often snaps up a catch, and is worth trying as the man comes
in ; otherwise a third slip up can hardly be spared.

If your wicket keeper is not likely to stump anyone, make a slip
of him, provided you play a short leg ; otherwise he is wanted at
the wicket for the single runs.

And if Point is no good as Point for a sharp catch, make a
field of him. A bad Point will make more catches, and save
more runs some yards back. Many a time have I seen both
Point and wicket keeper standing where they were by use. The
general must place his men not on any plan or theory, but where
each particular man's powers can be turned to the best account.
We have already mentioned the common error of men standing
too far to save one, and not as far as is compatible with saving
two.

Bowlers are not always good judges of play : the general should
observe how near the ball may be pitched to the batsmen respectively. Though, of course, it is a fatal error to worry the bowler by
too many directions.

With a free hitter, a man who does not pitch very far up answers
best ; short leg balls are not easily hit. A lobbing bowler, with the
longstop, and four men in all on the On side, will shorten the innings
of many a reputed fine hitter.

If a man will not play forward, pitch well up to him, and depend upon your slips.

A good arrangement of your men, according to these principles, will make eleven men do the work of thirteen. Some men play nervously at first they come in, so it is so much waste of your forces to lay your men far out, and equally a waste not to open your field as they begin to hit.

That cricket is partly a game of chance there can be no doubt ; but that all is chance that men call such, we strenuously deny. Young players should not think of being out by chance : there is a certain intuitive adaptation of play to circumstances, that, however seemingly impossible, will result from observation and experience, unless the idea of chance closes the eyes to instruction.

With these hints, we bid our brother cricketers adieu ; assuring them that we are ourselves by no means too old to learn ; that all information will be thankfully received ; and requesting, in the words of Horace—

> " . . . si quid novisti rectius istus
> Candidus imperti ; si non, his utere mecum."

ON JOHN MITFORD'S

Review of Nyren's
Young Cricketer's Tutor

⟨∾≫∾⟩

THE REVEREND JOHN MITFORD WAS WELL KNOWN IN HIS OWN time as " Sylvanus Urban " editor of *The Gentleman's Magazine,* but he is now almost solely remembered for his review of Nyren's *The Young Cricketer's Tutor* in that magazine—where it appeared unsigned and took no considerable place among the current reviews. Half of it appeared in the July issue of 1833 and then the rest of it was held over until September. Little or no credit beyond the title of the book is given to the proper quarter—Charles Cowden Clarke, (even his name misspelt,) is given as the author, and Nyren is not mentioned at all. Then for about five thousand words Mitford plagiarises Nyren and Clarke—turning their fine enthusiasm into an even greater fury which lacks the dignity and sometimes the point, of the original.

Perhaps the most valuable contribution made by Mitford's notice to the literature of cricket is the review of contemporary players of the early thirties. Even there Mitford might, to our benefit, have been more explicit. He does, however, tend to adjust the balance. Presumably Fennex concurred in his judgments which placed these later players—Pilch, Felix, Knatchbull, Harenc and others, on a level comparable with that of the great men of the Hambledon players. And Fennex, that great old player, Mitford's sheltering of whom can hardly be too kindly remembered by cricketers, would not have placed a later generation on a par with his own contemporaries without good cause. The section in which Mitford moves on to his own time was excluded from *The Hambledon Men* because it lay outside the scope of that book : it is included here because my aim is different and this passage adjusts historic perspective.

Mitford is the arch-enthusiast, and an arch-devotee of the rolling and classic-begotten phrase, the pompous sentence. His apostrophe of Lumpy is barely to be taken seriously but that of Pilch, his great idol, is laughable in the extreme, a classic of unintended humour.

Far too often Mitford smothers a not-too-clear point in a blanket of verbiage so that we are annoyed that he missed his opportunity of giving us a contemporary judgment which would now be of the utmost value. It should be remembered, however, that he passed to Pycroft much information which was embodied in *The Cricket Field*. A considerable amount of Mitford's gleanings from Fennex will be found in Pycroft's *Oxford Memories* in which cricket is again the dominant. Mitford sheltered Felix and he met Beldham and even the shreds which he left us about those two great players are to be cherished.

With the exceptions of a few annoying spelling errors and mannerisms Mitford's review is here reprinted exactly as it first appeared in *The Gentleman's Magazine*.

JOHN ARLOTT

REVIEW

BY

THE REV. JOHN MITFORD

THE YOUNG CRICKETER'S TUTOR

BY

CHARLES COWDEN[1] CLARKE

FROM

THE GENTLEMAN'S MAGAZINE, JULY 1833

[[1] *Gentleman's Magazine* misprinted " Conden " (ED.).]

The Young Cricketers Tutor

SOME OF THE MOST CELEBRATED WRITERS OF ANTIQUITY, WHOSE
names are illustrious as moralists, philosophers, and historians,
have not disdained to stoop from the lofty elevation of Science, to
discourse on the games, the field-sports, and the amusements of the
people. Xenophon left the conversation of Socrates to give instructions, and those minute and plain, on the management of hounds,
on the choice of their names, on the treatment of the pack, and on
the tactics of the chase. Arrian, the pupil of Epictetus, has also
bestowed on us a Treatise on Hunting, that may rival Mr. Beckford's
in accuracy, and far exceeds it in elegance. We have also a Greek
volume on Hawking, another on the Rod and Line ; though we
confess, that of the *piscatory* achievements of the ancients we have
no very high opinion,—perhaps no very clear knowledge. We take
it, that it was a rude kind of operation, sometimes in the way in
which our sailors fish for whitings :—what could it have been ?
Say, oh ! ye salmon-fishers of the Don, and of the Dee—when the
artificial fly was not known ! Now, it is not only that life wants
amusement just as much as it requires serious occupation ; and,
therefore, it is of importance what *kind* of amusement should be
pursued ; but it is also interesting to trace the species of amusement
into the habits and genius of the people. Thus, even an apparently
trifling inquiry becomes dignified by the manner of treating it,
and no unimportant part of Grecian history, of the rise of genius,
and of the progress of arts and the education of youth, is connected
with the immortal honours of the Isthmian and Olympian Games.
Some pursuits, like those of the field or of the river, seem common
to the people of every country : others arise from the peculiar
situation, or the habits and inclinations of the inhabitants. All the
nations in Europe are in some sense sportsmen ; the cry of the
hound, and the horn of the huntsman is heard from the Grampian

hills to the very granite steeps of Hæmus. The hare is coursed alike on the downs of Swafham and the arid plains of Isphan ; and the sound of the fatal and unerring rifle breaks the repose equally of the woods of Lochabar, and of the distant forests of Teflis. On the other hand, there are many pursuits and games that are confined within certain limits, and belong to a peculiar people. *Tennis* used to be the favourite pastime of the French. Shooting at the wooden bird, of the *Swiss*. *Ballone* is the magnificent and splendid diversion of the Italian nobles. *Skating* is the Dutchman's pleasure. And thus, *Cricket* is the pride and the privilege of the Englishman alone. Into this, his noble and favourite amusement, no other people ever pretended to penetrate : a Frenchman or a German would not know which end of a bat they were to hold ; and so fine, so scientific, and so elaborate is the skill regarding it, that only a small part of England have as yet acquired a knowledge of it. In this, *Kent* has always stood proudly pre-eminent ; Kent is emphatically the field of the cricketer's glory. Sussex, Hampshire, and Surrey, next follow in the list ; and Middlesex owes its present fame to the establishment of the Marylebone Club within its boundaries. Of late years an extension in the practice of the game has taken place ; and while Yorkshire justly plumes herself on the extraordinary accomplishment of *Marsden* ; the county of Norfolk holds aloft the hitherto unrivalled science and talents of *Pilch*.

To those who are curious in investigating the origin of Sports and Pastimes, it will be doubtless a matter of some astonishment to hear that familiar as the word *cricket* is now to their ears, it can be only traced back about one hundred years. The word first occurs in a song of Tom Durfey's, ' Of a noble race was Shenkin,' [1]

> " Hur was the prettiest fellow
> At football, or at *cricket*,
> At hunting chace, or thimble race,
> How featly hur could prick it."

The game itself, however, under some name or other, is of very high antiquity. The late Mr. Bonstetten of Geneva, we remember, traced it into *Iceland* ; it was certainly *British*. Its derivation is probably from the Saxon *cryce—a stick* ; and scientific and complicated and finished as it now is, it had its origin in the ancient amusement of *club and ball* ; [2] a rude and simple game.

We presume that, for more than half a century from the time that its name became celebrated in Durfey's song, cricket did not

[1] See " Pills to purge Melancholy."

[2] See Strutt's Sports and Pastimes, where some cuts are given from old pictures, missals, etc.

advance much in character as a dextrous or scientific game ; but remained the common sport or pastime of the Cuddys and Hobbinols, the boors of the country wakes and fairs.

It was somewhere between the years 1770 and 1780, that a great and decisive improvement took place, and that cricket first began to assume that truly skilful and scientific character which it now possesses. The pretty and sequestered village of Hambledon in Hants, was the nursery of the best players ; the down of Broad Halfpenny the arena of their glory,—the Marathon ennobled by their victories, and sometimes enriched with their blood.[1] At that time the Duke of Dorset and Sir Horace Mann were the great patrons and promoters of the game. Great as many of them were and deserving a more lasting fame than they have attained, the name of *John Small* shines out in pre-eminent lustre. Him followed *Brett*, the tremendous bowler, and *Barber* and *Hogsflesh*, whose bowling was also admirable,—they had a high delivery and certain lengths ; and he must be a more than common batter who can stand long against such confounding perplexities. *Tom Sueter* had the eye of an eagle, and a giant's paw ; and when he rushed in to meet the ball, his stroke was certain, decisive, and destructive. Off went the ball, as if fired from a gun ; and woe to those opposed to him in the game ! But we must hasten on.—These *great men* (for great they truly were !) have long been where sound of ball, or sight of bat, or shout of applauding friends, will never reach them again. They lie side by side in the church-yard of Hambledon, and many a sigh have we breathed over their peaceful graves. We must pass over *George Lear*, called ' Little George ' but great in every thing but stature ; and '*Edward Abarrow*,' who, nobody knows why—was always called ' Curry ' ; and *Peter Steward*, for his spruceness called ' Buck.' We cannot say ' they had no poet, and they died ' ; for their names are consecrated in the following lines :

" Buck, Curry, and Hogsflesh, Barber, and Brett,
   Whose swiftness in bowling was ne'er equall'd yet,
   I had almost forgot (they deserve a large bumper)
   Little George the long stop, and Tom Sueter the stumper."

Such were the chief heroes, the valour of those arms sustained the fate of the modern Troy ; but opposed to them are the names of enemies arrayed in formidable phalanx ! Come forth ! thou

[1] The blood of a cricketer is seldom, however, shed from any part of his body but his fingers ; but the fingers of an old cricketer, so scarred, so bent, so shattered, so indented, so contorted, so venerable ! are enough to bring tears of envy and emulation from any eye—we are acquainted with such a pair of hands, " if hands they may be called, that shape have none."

pride of Surrey ! thou prince of the ancient bowlers ! thou man of
iron nerve, and never-failing eye.   Come forth, *Tom Lumpy* ![1]
come forth from the well-filled cellar, and well-stored larder, of
thy first and greatest patron the Earl of Tankerville,—bring with
thee thy companions in fame, *Shock White*, and *Frame*, and *Johnny
Wood* and *Miller* the gamekeeper, whose eye was alike sure at a
woodcock or a ball.   Reader ! if thou hast any love or knowledge
of this noble game,—if thou hast any delight in traversing the
ancient fields of glory, or visiting the scenes of departed genius, or
hanging a slender wreath on the monument of men who deserved
a richer sepulchre,—shut your eyes for one moment to the follies
and vanities of passing events, and believe yourself walking in a
fine summer morning on the down of Broad Halfpenny, waiting the
commencement of a match.   You know the scenery of that secluded
vale ; the fine undulating sweep of its beechen forests, the beautiful
and variegated turf, the glittering of the ocean, the blue hills of the
Isle of Wight looming in the distance, and the elmy gardens and
half-wild orchards sprinkled in the bottom.   Well ! believe yourself
transported there ;—and now ten (the old hour, before modern
fashion and indolence had superseded it) has struck ; a few
cricketers in their white dress [2] and numerous groups of farmers and
rustics, have assembled from grange and farm, from Exton down
to the hills of Petersfield,—and now all is bustle and expectation.
A shout !—turn to the right ! You may instantly know who it is ;
Noah Mann from North Chapel in Sussex, who lately joined the
club, and who rides at least twenty miles every Tuesday to practise.
Look at those handkerchiefs on the ground ! Riding at full speed,
he stoops down, and collects every one without effort.   Mann was a
severe hitter.   One stroke of his is even now remembered, in which
he got the immense number of ten runs.   He was short, and black
as a gypsey, broad chest, large hips, and spider legs.   He never
played with a hat ; *his* complexion *benefited* by the Sun.   The roar
that followed Mann's celebrated hit never is to be forgotten, it was
like the rushing of a cataract ; it came pouring from a thousand
lungs.   And there is his namesake and opponent, Sir Horace, walking
about outside the ground cutting down the daisies with his stick,
as gentle he, as the simple flowers which he was strewing beside
him !—That stout, well-made man in with Mann is *James Alyward*,

[1] His real name was Stevens.

[2] The old cricketers were dressed differently from the modern.   The gentlemen
always played in breeches and silk stockings ; the players, as Lord Winchelsea's, wore
hats with gold binding, and ribbons of particular colour.   The present dress is inconvenient as well as unbecoming ; for trowsers may be in the way of the ball.   Mr. Budd
was the last cricketer who wore the old dress.

the farmer. Glory and honour be to him. Alyward once stood in two whole days, and scored a hundred and sixty-seven runs. Soon after, he was seen to have been called by Sir Horace Mann into a corner of the field ; a short conversation took place between them ; it was mysterious, in an under-tone, with short glances of circumspection ; but it was decisive : they soon parted ; and never after was James Aylward seen at the Hambledon Club. The next time he was arrayed, was among its opponents, and fighting under Sir Horace's banners. When Aylward affected grandeur, he used to call for a *lemon* after he had been in but a short time : this was a high piece of affection for a farmer,—it was a fine touch of the heroic. That man who now takes the bat, has not, perhaps nor ever will have, a superior. Stand up, *Tom Walker* ! show thy scraggy frame, thy apple-john face, thy spider-legs, thick at the ankles as at the hips, thy knuckles like the bark of the Hainault oak ! Tom had neither flesh, nor blood, nor skin. He was all muscle, tendon, gristle, covered with the hide of the rhinoceros. You might as well attempt to get Wellington from a field of battle, or Bentley from a Greek poet, as to get Tom from his wicket. Once Lord Frederick Beauclerk was bowling to him ; four fine length balls one after the other were sent in with his Lordship's finished science ; down they all went before the bat, and off went his Lordship's white hat, as usual, calling him " a confounded old beast."—" I doant care nothing whatsomeer ee zays," quoth Tom, and on he went, laying his Lordship down in the finest style and the coolest temper. Tom was a farmer, and his land lay near the Devil's Punch-bowl.

Next came *John Wells*, called " Honest *John Wells* ! " he was a baker at Farnham, a well-set man, short, and stout like a cob. He was a good bowler and steady batter, and a good servant of all work ; but we must hasten on, for we are at length arrived at the tent of *Achilles* himself. Stop, reader, and look, if thou art a cricketer, with reverence and awe on that venerable and aged form ! These are the remains of the once great, glorious, and unrivalled *William Beldham,* called for love and respect, and for his flaxon locks and his fair complexion, " Silver Billy." Beldham was a close set, active man, about five feet eight inches. Never was such a player ! so safe, so brilliant, so quick, so circumspect ; so able in counsel, so active in the field ; in deliberation so judicious, in execution so tremendous. It mattered not to him who bowled, or how he bowled, fast or slow, high or low, straight or bias ; away flew the ball from his bat, like an eagle on the wing. It was a study for Phidias to see Beldham rise to strike ; the grandeur of the attitude, the settled

composure of the look, the piercing lightning of the eye, the rapid
glance of the bat, were electrical. Men's hearts throbbed within
them, their cheeks turned pale and red. Michael Angelo should
have painted him. Beldham was great in every hit, but his peculiar
glory was the *cut*. Here he stood with no man beside him, the laurel
was all his own ; it was like the cut of a *racket*. His wrist seemed to
turn on springs of the finest steel. He took the ball, as Burke did
the House of Commons, between wind and water ; not a moment
too soon or late. Beldham still survives. He lives near Farnham ;
and in his kitchen, black with age, but, like himself, still untouched
with worms, hangs the trophy of his victories ; the delight of his
youth, the exercise of his manhood, and the glory of his age—his
BAT. Reader ! believe me, when I tell you I trembled when I
touched it ; it seemed an act of profaneness, of violation. I pressed
it to my lips, and returned it to its sanctuary.

The last, the " Ultimus Romanorum," we can find room to
commemorate, is *David Harris*. Who knows not David Harris ? the
finest *bowler* whom the world ever rejoiced in when living, or
lamented over when dead. Harris was by trade a potter, and lived
at Odiham in Hants, an honest, plain-faced (in two senses), worthy
man. " Good David Harris " he was called ; of strict principle,
high honour, inflexible integrity ; a character on which scandal
or culumny never dared to breathe. A good cricketer, like a good
orator, must be an honest man ; but what are orators compared
to the men of cricket. There have been a hundred, a thousand
orators ; there never was but one David Harris. Many men can
make good speeches, but few men can deliver a good ball. Many
men can throw down a strong enemy, but Harris could overthrow
the strongest wicket. Cicero once undermined the conspiracy of
Catiline ; and Harris *once* laid prostrate even the stumps of Beldham.

It is said that it is utterly impossible to convey with the pen an
idea of the grand effect of Harris's bowling. His attitude, when
preparing to deliver the ball, was masculine, erect, and appalling.
First, he stood like a soldier at drill, upright. Then with a graceful
and elegant curve, he raised the fatal ball to his forehead, and
drawing back his right foot, started off. Woe be to the unlucky
wight who did not know how to stop these cannonades ! his fingers
would be ground to dust against the bat, his bones pulverized, and
his blood scattered over the field. Lord F. Beauclerk has been
heard to say, that Harris's bowling was one of the grandest sight
in the universe. Like the Pantheon, in Akenside's Hymn, it was
" simply and severely great." Harris was terribly afflicted with

the gout ; it was at length difficult for him to stand ; a great armchair was therefore always brought into the field, and after the delivery of the ball, the hero sat down in his own calm and simple grandeur, and reposed. A fine tribute this, to his superiority, even amid the tortures of disease !

If, like Sallust and Hume, we may venture our comparison of the relative merits of two illustrious men, we should say, in contrasting Harris with Lumpy, that,

Harris always chose a ground when pitching a wicket, where his ball would *rise*. Lumpy endeavoured to gain the advantage of a declivity where his might *shoot*.

Harris considered his partner's wicket as carefully as his own. Lumpy attended only to himself.

Lumpy's ball was as well pitched as Harris's, but delivered *lower*, and never got up so high. Lumpy was also a pace or two slower.

Lumpy gained more wickets than Harris ; but then fewer notches were got from Harris's bowling : and more players were caught out. Now and then a great batter as Fennex, or Beldham, would beat Lumpy entirely ; but Harris was always great, and always to be feared.

We must now draw our brief memoirs to a close. Unwillingly do we drop the pen. Very pleasant has our task been, delightful our recollections. Farewell, ye smiling fields of Hambledon and Windmill Hill ! Farewell ye thymy pastures of our beloved Hampshire, and farewell ye spirits of the brave, who still hover over the fields of your inheritance. Great and illustrious eleven ! fare ye well ! in these fleeting pages at least, your names shall be enrolled. What would life be, deprived of the recollection of you ? Troy has fallen, and Thebes is a ruin. The pride of Athens is decayed, and Rome is crumbling to the dust. The philosophy of Bacon is wearing out ; and the victories of Marlborough have been overshadowed by fresher laurels. All is vanity but CRICKET ; all is sinking in oblivion but you. Greatest of all elevens, fare ye well !

Sacred to the memory of the eleven greatest players of the Hambledon Club.

1. David Harris.	7. Tom Walker.
2. John Wells.	8. * —— Robinson.
3. * —— Purchase.	9. Noah Mann.
4. William Beldham.	10. * —— Scott.
5. John Small, jun.	11. * —— Taylor.
6. Harry Walker.	

[* see footnote p. 43 (Ed.)]

[1] That the scientific display of Cricket we now see, was not made till about the time of the *Great Men* whom we lately recorded, is clear for this reason ; that we can trace to *them* most of the fine *inventive* parts of the science.   *Tom Walker* laid down a bail ball, in a style peculiarly his own, and that all have since attempted to follow.   *Beldham* was the first person who *cut* the same kind of ball, and therefore made an improvement on the former plan ; for he obtained some runs, while the former was merely content to stop the ball.   That fine accomplished old cricketer *Fennex* has often (as we sat together in a winter evening over our gin and water, discoursing even till the morning star appears, on our beloved science), I say he has often told us, that *he* was the first person who ever went in and laid down a ball before it had time to rise to the bail.   And we have been much amused by his informing us of the astonishment and indignation of his father, who was a good old batsman, when he first beheld this innovation.   " Hey ! hey ! boy ! what is this ? do you call that play ? "   But he soon became sensible of the safety and excellence of the practice ; which saves alike the fingers and the wickets from a first-rate top-bailer. *Sueter* was the first wicket-keeper ; that part of the game having not been attended to before ; and we *believe* that *Boxall* was the first who by a turn of the wrist gave his balls a twist to the wicket.   *Freemantle* brought the province of *longstop* at once to perfection, never suffering a ball to pass, and covering a great deal of ground.   There were some good men besides these. *Boorman*, and *Booker*, and *Ring*, and *Purchase*, and *Clifford* (the last excellent as a bowler), and *Crosoer*, *cum multis aliis*.   The match is even now remembered when the predecessors of these men, the old players (including the elder Small), were brought against the *improved* Hambledon school, and beaten in a masterly and decisive manner.

Some of Tom Walker's scores about 1786, were superb.   In a match played against Kent and White Conduit Club (which was the father of the Marylabonne), Tom scored the amazing number of 95 runs in his first innings, and brought his bat out with him ; in the second he gained 102.   *Beldham's* name first appears on the 20th June, 1787, on the side of England, against the White Conduit Club, with six picked men.   In his second innings he obtained 63 runs.   Beldham never could keep his bat, his eyes, or his legs still ; and he was generally run out, as in this instance.   He would get 20 runs, while *Tom Walker* got 2, though they scored pretty

[1] Commencement of September section of review.

Figure 15. George Osbaldeston, M.P. (1787 – 1866), a
notable cricketer and all-round sportsman.

Figure 16. North-east view of the cricket grounds at Darnall, near Sheffield, 1827.

even at the end. *Harry Walker* [1] was also very quick in getting up
his score ; but not so safe as his illustrious brother, whom he
imitated, reverenced, and loved.   In looking over carefully the list
of matches for twenty years, we shall find no scores on the average
at all approaching those of the elder *Walker* and *Beldham* ; thus
clearly evincing their superiority.   But we must hasten on in our
narrative, and reluctantly close the gates of history on these two
unrivalled men. *Beldham's* name appeared for the *last time* in a
match played in Lord's Ground, on the 23rd July, 1821, of the
Players of England against the Club.   It was a match dignified by
the fine play of *Begley*, who gained 113 runs without being out.
Beldham brought away his bat garlanded with the victories of forty
years, with a score of 23, and his innings still unfinished.   *Tom
Walker* resigned the combat on the 25th of June, 1812, on Highdown
Hill in Sussex.   Other's names had appeared ; his old compeers,
the veterans by whose side he had so long frowned, stamped, and
grunted,[2] were gone ; and it is a relief to us to see his disappear ;
how we should shudder to read the speeches of William Pitt, and
Charles Fox, in answer to Messrs. Hume, Cobbett, and Faithfull ;
to see their names in conjunction, would be profanation ; the same
chamber could not hold them ; they ought not to speak the same
language.   Madame Vestris, or Mrs. Honey (Honey sweeter than
the sweetest produce of Narbonne), might as well be shut up in a
cage with monkeys, as the son of Chatham stand by the side of
Messrs. Evans and Warburton ; or the old hero of Hambledon
rank with the Ladbrokes and Lowthers of modern days.

  Fennex, who (thank God !) is still alive, and who at 76 will
bring down any wicket that is not carefully guarded, has been
providentially preserved to show us what the *ante-Homeric* heroes
were.   He was the first single wicket-player of his day ; for his
bat and ball were equally to be dreaded.   He beat at one innings
the *three* Mitcham players, who had beat Robinson.   He slew
Hector who had vanquished Patroclus.   His batting was (say *is*) as
elegant and strong ; his knowledge of every point of play complete.

  [1] Harry Walker was a left-handed player ; so was Harris, Freemantle, Aylward,
Brazier, and Clifford ; so that they had some fine *bowlers* among them. At this day,
our left-handed *batters* are superb ; but they have no *bowlers* of eminence. It is however
proposed to make a match of the *left-handed* against all England, next July. There is a
glory accompanying the names of all. Mills of Kent, Hayward of Cambridge, Marsden,
Searle, lead the van.

  [2] Tom Walker would never speak to any one, or give any answer when he was in
at the wicket. His tongue was tied, as his soul and body were surrendered to the struggle.
But he used to give such a *grunt*, if perchance a shooting ball was too quick for him and
brought him down, as I have heard described to be very like that of a broken-winded
horse, only of a deeper bass.

His fielding was astonishing in its activity, and in the space of ground he could cover ; and his bowling was far more swift and tremendous than even Harris's. We would back him for a score of balls (for his age will not let him continue) against any bowler in England. Reader ! do not be affronted ! but you, whoever you are, married, or in single blessedness, have no idea of the real comfort of a winter evening fire-side. In vain you talk of the pleasure of your dear young wife, and your pretty children (a boy and girl), and your *good* old aunt, good on account of her *will*, and your cat and cigar, and your Pope Joan and your elder wine. No ! believe me it won't do. Peep through the shutter of my snug parlour, and behold me and envy. There is the small oak table (it is now nine), with the pint of Geneva and the jug of hot water, and the snuff-box smiling on it. One cricket-bat, the practice one, lies on the small horse-hair sofa, as occasionally necessary for examplifications, and Harry Bentley's volume of the matches is open beside it. Do you see him ? the master of the field. There he sits, mark his animation! his gesture ! he is telling of a catch he made above 50 years since, and the ball is again in the air. He was taken instantly up to the Duchess of Richmond, of whose side he was, and she made a handicap of 6 guineas for him. She won hundreds by it. How my heart throbs, and my eyes glisten, and in what fearful suspense I sit, when he calls to life the ghost of a magnificent hit, fresh as the life, though half a century has intervened. I see the ball running at Moulsey Hurst, that fetched ten runs off Beldham's bat in 1787, as plainly as if it were in my own field. Then the trick he played *Butler Danvers*, when he came into the field dressed as a countryman, and was taken in *unconsciously*, merely to fill up the eleven ;—the sly look of Lord Winchelsea, as sly and as black as a gypsey's (the Finches were all black), (it had been planned between them) ; his delight, when they sent him down to the tent, to select whatever dress he chose to wear : his joy, when he heard " Countryman, you take the bat to begin with," and the consternation among the enemy's forces, when eighty notches were scored by him. You should hear of the day, when Manchester saw the flower of youth fall before him ; when he might have won *thousands*, if he had had them to stake. Or that single combat (nor Europe nor Asia ever beheld such, never seen from the Sigæan promontory, or on the banks of Simois) that even now (twice twenty years have passed since) will alone immortalize the plains of Wisbech. Midnight sounds in vain. Politics, scandal, Tories, Whigs, my Lord Grey, and the Bishop of Peterborough, and the last story about the Maids

of Honour, and Lady Farquhar's splendid breakfast, and the
unknown tongues, all solicit attention in vain ; they seem as
nothing, idle all and without interest ; one wonders how the world
can trouble itself about such toys. We fill the tumblers anew ;
and for the hundredth time I ask, " What was young *Small's*
favourite hit ? How did *John Wells* get his runs ? " Behold the
advantage, ye parents, of bringing up your sons (why not your
daughters ?) to the love of subjects which cannot be exhausted,
which never tire.

But we must hasten on.—The first time I see *Lord Fred. Beauclerk's*
name, is on the 2nd June, 1791. He played with Marylebourn
against Kent. Fennex and his Lordship bowled, and they beat
their adversaries by one innings and 113 runs ; in fact, it appears
by the score, that *Fennex, Beauclerk*, and *Beldham*, got out the whole
field between them. For thirty years after this, his Lordship stood
as the most accomplished cricketer in England. In batting he was
brought up in the school of Beldham, and he was quite as fine. He
introduced a slow home-and-easy kind of bowling, which was very
effective ; till Saunders and Begley, and the new players, destroyed
it, by rushing in, and driving it away. Though his Lordship has
given up the bat some years, we have seen enough of his practice
to say that his execution was eminently beautiful, and certainly not
equalled now.

Excepting the name of *Hammond*, the famous wicket-keeper, *Ray*
(a good batter) among the players, and those of *Tufton, Col. Upton*,
and *Bligh*, among the gentlemen, the old list of players remained
much the same, till about the year 1804.[1] Then the name of
Aislabie (the father of cricket, 'and the great *fautor* of the Marlabonne
Club) and of *Budd*, first appear. The latter gentleman resigned last
year, after near thirty years' display of the finest science ; and his
departure is much lamented. His fielding was excellent, his hits
strong and scientific ; but his bowling, once good, was no longer
of avail. A little before this the name of *Lambert* first appears among
those of the players. Take him in every department of the game,
we believe he has been esteemed as the *first player* that ever appeared.
His batting was straighforward, and driving, a good deal resembling
that of Mr. Ward ; who appears to have been instructed by him.
His bowling was excellent, and had a considerable twist. A
splendid single wicket match appears, in 1806, to have been played
by him, Robinson, and Beldham, against Bennet, Fennex, and

[1] Howard, Sparkes, and H. Bentley, are playing about this time. The bowling of
the first was very good, and lasted till lately in reputation, it was swift and straight.
Slater was the wicket keeper.

Lord F. Beauclerk, and won by the former. The play must have been very fine, for from 116 hits Lambert obtained only 13 runs.

The name of *Ashby*, which is seen in the lists of 1807, seems to connect us with modern times ; and we pause for a moment to remind our readers of the changes which are now taking place in one material branch of the game.

It appears, that however skilful or successful *bowlers* may be, they will in the long run be beaten by the *batter* ; as he becomes gradually accustomed to their balls, and knows how to meet them ; on this account the wickets were raised from 22 inches to 27, and proportionably altered in width. They had been once before-hand elevated on a similar account. But batters, notwithstanding, were so skilful, and the matches consequently lasted so long, that a new *system* of bowling was at length introduced. We have mentioned that *Boxall* and *Lumpy*, and other old bowlers, had a *twist* in their balls, which much increased the difficulty of meeting them ; but this was effected by a turn of the fingers or the wrist. *Ashby*, however, (who was brought up out of Kent, we believe, by Mr. Wills,) introduced the *round* bowling, by throwing the arm in a sweeping circular position. This puzzled the batsman much ; and the once-triumphant wickets fell before him. *Mathews* adopted the same system with equal success ; and we have seen these two bowlers clear off the batters in quick succession. They had however the same defect, they were too slow ;[1] they gave too much time ; and they were at length beaten like their predecessors. To them has succeeded the eminent projectors of the ball of the present day, whose merits we shall briefly recognize. *Lillywhite* stands first and foremost ; his balls are sent at a good pace, and come quickly off the ground[2]. They are well pitched ; generally straight to the wicket, and are very destructive. *Broadbridge* is more variable and irregular, and used much *finesse* about his play, which often succeeds ; but his bowling is in great request. He has gone off in batting surprisingly.

Cobbett, who is the Marylebourn bowler, has been for the last few seasons very successful ; his balls are slower than Lillywhite's, but have a very perplexing bias, and require a most accomplished batter to meet them.

[1] The plan adopted by good batters against slow *bias* bowling was successful ; if the ball pitched straight they played it ; if to the leg they placed the *left* leg before the wicket, extended the right, and struck the ball to the *left*, which often brought four or five runs ; and if they missed the ball they were by the laws of Cricket not out. This is Mr. Knatchbull's favourite hit. It of course is more difficult as the speed of the ball increases, but it rendered Mathews's bowling nugatory. Mr. *Budd* would jump before his wicket and cut him to pieces.

[2] *Pilch* has batted so long to Lillywhite, that he may be said to be perfectly master of his balls.

Begley of the Marylebourn Club is a good bowler and player generally, but is not sufficiently brought forward : he is generally umpire. *Burt* used to bowl very successfully ; his balls were very high, but too slow.

Pilch generally bowls in the matches, but he is inferior to the above.

Among the gentlemen two bowlers are to be found of the highest eminence. Mr. *Harenc's* balls are magnificent ; getting up and puzzling the unfortunate man who has to meet them ; and the bowling of Mr. *Mynn*, when he can get his balls less wide, will almost defy opposition ; the tremendous force at which they perform their journey, alone will bring destruction with it. Mr. *Jenner* seldom takes the ball now ; he had great success, but his bowling we think was not always fair.[1] We are convinced that the present style of bowling will never again fall back into the straight old under-hand mode ; but we hope also that it will not advance into *throws*, to which it is approaching ; and which, if allowed, will destroy the game altogether. The alteration in the manner of bowling also produced a change in the style of batting ; and an *old* batter would have much to learn were he to come now into the field. As the present style of bowling is wider from the wicket than the old, hitting to the leg, and the off-cut, are necessary parts of the batter's science ; without them he would score but few runs. *Cauldecourt*, though a good player, has never mastered the present system of bowling ; and the batting of Mr. *Ward* is far more adapted to meet the balls that were in vogue in the time when he first appeared.

About the year 1806 will be found the names of the great players of the present day, gradually appearing in the lists. Mr. *Brand*, *Bayley*, and *Lillywhite* ; and *Slater*, the wicket-keeper. Then *Bowyer* and *Brown*, of Brighton,[2] and at length in 1820, in the renowned match of Norfolk against Marylabonne, (when Mr. Ward scored the highest number that ever was remembered, viz. 278 in one innings) for the first time appears the name of *Fuller Pilch* ; then

[1] The law in bias bowling is that the *hand should not be above the elbow*, which is meant to keep it clear from a throw ; but that law is forever broken. Lillywhite and Cobbett both throw ; and Mr. Mynn's is, we think, a direct violation of the law in another way. Mr. *Jenner's* was often a jerk ; in fact the law now is conventional ; if every ball was stopped by the umpire that was not fair, the bowlers would all be put out, and very likely give up.

[2] *Brown* was a tremendous under-hand bowler. I remember at a single wicket match at Lord's, his bowling Searle, Saunders, and Broadbridge out without a run. He once told old Beldham that he would do the same to him. " I suppose," said Billy, " you will let me have this little bit of stick in my hand," pointing to his bat. He went in, and fetched 70 against him. Brown's batting is very common, and depends upon force.

the names of *Searle, Jenner, Saunders,* and others, shining forth, like stars one by one brightening in the heavens, which brings us down to our present day.

Among the *players* we recollected none whose brilliancy of stroke, and quickness of movement, and elegance of style, delighted us more than that of *Saunders.* "We better could have spared a better man." What business had consumption and hectic fevers to come into the cricket field to take him away ? Poor fellow ! we saw him in his last match. His cheek was hollow and his lips pale, but his execution was as fine as ever. His *cut to the point* was unrivalled, and his *leg hit* very powerful and sure.

His brother-in-law, *Searle,* a few years since stood as the champion of England. He has played but little lately, having engagements in business which he will not (why will he not ?) neglect at Godalming. We saw him, however, once this year at Marylebourn, and were much pleased. His *cuts* too were masterly.

Begley is growing old, and his batting is not suited to the present style of bowling ; he can no longer insure his 90 and 100 runs, as he used to do in fine style ; but he has been a first-rate player ; he has a style of batting peculiarly his own, and as a fieldsman he is invincible.

Marsden bears a great name in Yorkshire. As a fieldsman he is the finest at *point* we can conceive ; as a batter he gets his runs very quick, is very vigorous and decisive, but he runs in too much off his ground, and is wanting in temper and judgment and discretion ; however he is a good player, and had he been brought up at Marylebourn, among fine players, would have been eminent.

Wenman is a great favourite at present ; he keeps wicket excellently, bats very finely, with great judgment, and is a very steady and accomplished player.

The greatest name we have reserved to the last. Come forth from thy public-house at the bottom of Surrey Hill, Norwich, which thou keepest, with thy sister as thy bar-maid, *Fuller Pilch* ! fresh from thy late victory over the pride of Sheffield ! Pilch is undoubtedly a very fine player, and would have been hugged with delight by old Tom Walker, if he could have seen his style of batting. As a single wicket-player he is indisputably the first man of his day ; he may be backed against any man safely for runs ; he plays more *forward* than any other player, which he can do from his length of arm ; therefore he does not *cut,* which indeed he never did, nor did his masters, Fennex and Robinson, whose style he has adopted.

Figure 17. Lord's Cricket Ground, engraved by Stalker from a painting by Laporte, commissioned by *The Sporting Magazine*, 1835.

Among the gentlemen, we think Mr. *Ward* is declining *this* year in his play, though last year we thought him excellent ; but he is getting too lusty for an exercise which requires so much activity. Mr. *Jenner* plays but little, but his style is very superior. He is not only the finest wicket-keeper in England of the present day, but the finest that ever was ; no one else approaches him. Mr. *Harenc* bats elegantly ; we have already spoken of his bowling. A gentleman of Blackheath, who plays under the name of Felix, we think has no superior ; his play is in the most finished manner, and gives universal delight. There is not much to be said in favour of Messrs. *Kinaston, Woodhouse,* or *Romilly,* when the bowling is first-rate ; and *Col. Lowther* and *Lords Strathaven* and *Clonblock* ought to play in *private,* especially the Colonel, who was designed rather to stand for the *stumps* than to hold a *bat.*

We therefore close with the name of a gentleman whom we think to be at present the first batter in the Marylebourn Club,— we mean the *Reverend Mr. Knatchbull.* He has won his way by indefatigable practice and attention, and love of the game, into the eminence he well deserves. He is now a very safe wicket, and a very strong and scientific hitter ; his leg-hits are very fine, and quite in a style of his own ; as a fieldsman he is in the very first rank. We hope and trust that his professional engagements in Norfolk will never detain the Reverend gentleman from the classical ground of Marylabonne. A curate can easily supply his place in the church, but who is to supply it in the field ? We shall miss his black unhooded head, his red shining face, and his all but shirtless body. He ought to have the living of St. John's Wood, when he could play and preach alternately. Could it not be obtained ? There are some exceedingly good players who occasionally appear on the field, such as *Mr. Partridge* of Norfolk, *Lord Grimston, Mr. Sivewright,* among the gentlemen ; and *Llanaway* and *Wells* and *Box,* among the players ; and some very bad ones, who too often are seen, as *Sir V. Cotton, Mr. Caldwell,* etc. But we have already exceeded our limits.—We must turn to graver subjects and wiser deliberations. October is coming, and we must hang up our willow bats ; and with them all the delightful recollections they command ; till the swallow comes again, and the Messrs. Dark have ordered the ground to be rolled, and our old friend *Goule* appears riding from Kensington with the first rose in his button-hole, sleek and smiling, and as *good* as the bats he brings into the field.

The epitaph of the period may lie in that of one of its towering figures, Alfred Mynn, hop farmer, fast bowler and mighty hitter. It is itself a period piece, written by William Jeffrey Prowse (1836—1870) not to be ranked as poetry but technically sound and high in the levels of folk verse, celebrating a popular hero in popular terms. Its last stanza is well known; its full, naïvely romantic quality emerges in the entire piece.

IN MEMORIAM, ALFRED MYNN

Jackson's pace is very fearful; Willshire's hand is very high:
William Caffyn has good judgement, and an admirable eye:
Jemmy Grundy's cool and clever, almost always on the spot:
Tinsley's slows are often telling, though they sometimes
    catch it hot.
But however good their trundling—pitch, or pace, or break,
    or spin—
Still the monarch of all bowlers, to my mind, was Alfred
    Mynn.

Richard Daft is cool and cautious with his safe and graceful
    play;
If George Griffith gets a loose one, he can send it far away.
You may bowl your best at Hayward, and whatever style you
    try
Will be vanquished by the master's steady hand and certain
    eye.
But whatever fame and glory these and other bats may win,
Still the monarch of hard hitters, to my mind, was Alfred
    Mynn.

You may praise the pluck of Burbidge, as he plays an uphill
    march;
You may thunder cheers to Miller, for a wondrous running
    catch;
You may join with me in wishing that the Oval once again
Shall resound with hearty plaudits to the praise of Mr. Lane;
But the gentlemen of England the match will hardly win
Till they find another bowler, such as glorious Alfred Mynn.

When the great old Kent Eleven, full of pluck and hope
    began
The grand battle with All England, single-handed, man to
    man,
How the hop-men watched their hero, massive, muscular, and
    tall,
As he mingled with the players, like a king among them all;
Till to some old Kent enthusiasts it would almost seem a sin
To doubt their county's triumph when led on by Alfred Mynn.

Though Sir Frederick and "The Veteran" bowled straight
    and sure and well,
Though Box behind the wicket only Lockyer can excel;
Though Jemmy Dean, as long-stop, would but seldom grant
    a bye;
Though no novices in batting were George Parr and Joseph
    Guy—
Said the fine old Kentish farmers, with a fine old Kentish grin,
"Why, there ain't a man among them as can match our Alfred
    Mynn".

And whatever was the issue of the frank and friendly fray.
(Aye, and often has his bowling turned the fortunes of the
    day),
Still the Kentish men fought bravely, never losing hope or
    heart,
Every man of the Eleven glad and proud to play his part.
And with five such mighty cricketers, 'twas but natural to
    win,
As Felix, Wenman, Hillyer, Fuller Pilch, and Alfred Mynn.

With his tall and stately presence, with his nobly moulded
    form,
His broad hand was ever open, his brave heart was ever warm;
All were proud of him, all loved him. As the changing seasons
    pass,
As our champion lies a-sleeping underneath the Kentish grass,
Proudly, sadly will we name him—to forget him were a sin.
Lightly lie the turf upon thee, kind and manly Alfred Mynn!
WILLIAM JEFFREY PROWSE

On the Cricket Classics

NYREN, PYCROFT AND MITFORD TAKE US FROM 1776 TO 1850 : they are so outstandingly the leading cricket writers of that long era—almost a third of the period of recorded cricket—that they must be regarded as essential reading in the history of the game. Their work has qualities which suit it also to those concerned with the more literary aspect. In the latter respect the extent to which both Pycroft and Mitford inherit from Nyren detracts from them only in so far as his influence dominates their approach. More important from the historical point of view is the way in which he influences their perspective. So strongly has the imaginative quality of the sketches of the Hambledon players seized upon both of them that, as soon as they move on to the subsequent period, their writing looses force and the impression on the reader is less deep.

The importance of the period following Hambledon is most apparent in Pycroft although there only by implication. Under the heading " A Dark Chapter in the Game " he records the superficial facts of a phase the importance of which is barely recognized in the text. During those sixty years between the decline of Hambledon and the rise of the All-England Eleven, the character of cricket in England changed completely. The alterations in the laws which attempted to give the bowler some degree of equality with the ever-growing power of the batsman are well-known : the change in general character is rarely so widely stressed. (This is probably due to the fact that writers on cricket are studying the game from close quarters and incline to detail.) To say that the change made cricket no longer an excuse for huge wagers and bribes is to stress its negative side which was, in fact, a product of the positive side. This positive aspect was the imposition of the Victorian attitude upon the sport. Cricket has always been so close to the people—despite repeated, misguided and unsuccessful attempts to confine it—that it has reflected the changes in the social life of England. As the educated, enquiring, Victorian mind applied itself to cricket, it tended to make the game increasingly scientific ; bribery and betting, which might have interfered with the process, became not only morally reprehensible but also an obstruction to the course which the game was taking. This latter fact tended to produce more general acquiescence and rapid action in the eradication of these practices. Certainly this transitional phase lacks the colour of Hambledon, or the high excitement of the great Test rubbers of modern days and it is this fact which has led to the neglect of nineteenth century cricket. If we ignore development and look for isolated events of importance, the most important facet of the time was emergence and the triumphal march of the great Kent eleven of the thirties. Here, too, the individual excellence of Mynn, Felix, Pilch and Wenman (whom other single cricketers have equalled) seems to have been contemporarily more highly esteemed than the eleven which contained them and other great players—an eleven which, even against the entire history of cricket, seems still to have been the greatest of all county teams. We must appreciate that Pycroft and Mitford had neither the backward-looking range and resultant nostalgic romanticism of Nyren, nor our wider historic perspective. We must regard their writing, when they deal with their own time, as no more than valuable contemporary chronicles. We shall do well to be grateful for them, to accept their enthusiasm and their contemporary judgments, but not their wider appraisals.

Nyren wrote of a game which was restricted both geographically and socially, but Pycroft, coming later, saw, without always appreciating its significance, the age of change.

Pycroft wrote at the end of one and the beginning of another of the important phases in the history of cricket—at the beginning of one which has been insufficiently documented. This was the period of William Clarke's All-England Eleven. Here yet another facet of Victorian mentality makes itself apparent—the missionary urge. If Clarke's motives in forming and organizing this famous team were less altruistic than those of the religious, social and political missionaries of his time, the mentality which supported them was not.

Because of the further era of new development on whose threshold Pycroft stood, the period which these three men recorded can never be repeated. The All-England Eleven, by spreading cricket up and down the country and into the remotest hamlet, made the rise of another Hambledon or another Kent eleven of the thirties impossible.

Never again can a village challenge and beat all England ; never again can there be such concentration of talent, never again can "England" be two districts and a city. If that period is gone, we must, nevertheless be grateful that it was as it was. The very restriction, geographical and social, to which I have referred, was a boon to the eventual spreading of the game in that it made certain that the sport was matured before it spread. The maturity was to a desirable state : had cricket gone, half-formed, to various parts of England the differing regional character must inevitably have moulded it into varying forms too contrasted to be reconcilable. But Slindon, the Farnham of the immortal ginger-bread baker, Harry Hall, Broadhalfpenny Down, Windmill Down, Homerton, Sevenoaks Vine, Montpelier, the Lord's ground of Thomas Lord (i.e. prior to its passing to Dark in 1836) were substantially the same nursery, growing the same plant.

This was the great advantage which Clarke's " missionaries " held : they preached a mature belief, demonstrated a mature craft ; they moved with certainty because their experience was securely grounded in tradition and practice.

The unity of the works of these three writers, their fitness for inclusion in a single volume, is most apparent in historic perspective but identity of spirit also makes them sympathetic neighbours. This identity of spirit is the more remarkable when we realize the immense differences between the three men. Nyren was an eighteenth-century country yeoman, limited by economics to the culture of the parish church rather than of the Grand Tour.

Mitford inherited the wide culture of the eighteenth-century cleric : he simultaneously animated it with the spirit of " Lyrical Ballads " and diluted it with the materialism of the Industrial Revolution : he is William Lisle Bowles midway in transition to Martin Tupper.

Pycroft had the acceptance of change without full perception which was typical of the mid-Victorian era : he toyed with history to his own delight rather than serve it to the satisfaction of later historians.

Together they take the game from the seed-bed of Hambledon to planting-out in the formal gardens of Lords. The inspiration, making, seeding and flowering of other plots throughout the world, with Lord's as their Kew Gardens was still to come—but already it was inevitable.

The cricket writing of the later period was to be of a very different character. The factual documentation of Haygarth's

Cricket Scores and Biographies, the semi-scientific, technical approach of Felix and others was to be even more truly Victorian. A yet more self-consciously prosperous age was to produce Ranjitsinhji's *Jubilee Book of Cricket* (an outstandingly brilliant text which is rarely valued as highly as it should be) and the erudite analysis of C. B. Fry. The study of cricket reached the present generation before the sensitive and scholarly *History of Cricket* of H. S. Altham was both demanded and provided, to stand as pre-eminent in its proportion, knowledge and care. Only of recent years, after a gap of a century has the game produced, in Neville Cardus, a worthy successor to Nyren.

Yet the reader and the writer of cricket books will do well to realize, as any dispassionate literary critic does, that cricket has still to produce a work of comparable magnitude to Izaak Walton's *The Compleat Angler*. That is the goal at which these cricket classics aim, to which, in falling short of it, they continue to point the way.